D0152120

Psychoanalytic Approaches With the Hostile and Violent Patient

Psychoanalytic Approaches With the Hostile and Violent Patient

Herbert S. Strean
Editor

The Haworth Press
New York

Psychoanalytic Approaches With the Hostile and Violent Patient has also been published as *Current Issues in Psychoanalytic Practice,* Volume 1, Number 2, Summer 1984.

© 1984 by The Haworth Press, Inc. All rights reserved. No part of this work may be reproduced or utilized in any form or by any means, electronic or mechanical including photocopying, microfilm and recording, or by any information storage and retrieval system, without permission in writing from the publisher. Printed in the United States of America.

The Haworth Press, Inc., 28 East 22 Street, New York, NY 10010

Library of Congress Cataloging in Publication Data
Main entry under title:

Psychoanalytic approaches with the hostile and violent patient.

"Has also been published as Current issues in psychoanalytic practice, volume 1, number 2, summer 1984"—T.p. verso.
Includes bibliographical references.
1. Violence—Addresses, essays, lectures. 2. Violence—Etiology—Addresses, essays, lectures. 3. Psychoanalysis—Addresses, essays, lectures. 4. Psychotherapist and patient—Addresses, essays, lectures. I. Strean, Herbert S. [DNLM: 1. Psychoanalytic therapy. 2. Violence. 3. Hostility. WM 460.6 P9733]
RC569.5.V55P79   1984   616.85'82   84-3784
ISBN 0-86656-319-9

Psychoanalytic Approaches With the Hostile and Violent Patient

Current Issues in Psychoanalytic Practice
Volume 1, Number 2

CONTENTS

A LETTER FROM THE EDITOR   1
    Herbert S. Strean

From Hostility to Violence: Some Clinical Observations   3
    Reuben Fine

The "Seeds" of Murder as Sown "in the Nursery"   19
    Lucy Freeman

Terrorizing the Analyst   29
    Sidney M. Rosenblatt

Self Defense: Multiple Personality and the Fear of Murder 35
    Robert N. Mollinger

Aggression Victimology: Treatment of the Victim   47
    Irwin L. Kutash

Robert Lindner and the Case of Charles: A Teen-Age Sex
  Murderer: "Songs My Mother Taught Me"   65
    Robert C. Lane

EDITOR

HERBERT S. STREAN, D.S.W.

HONORARY EDITOR

REUBEN FINE. Ph.D.

ASSOCIATE EDITOR

LUCY FREEMAN

ADMINISTRATIVE ASSOCIATE TO THE EDITOR

JOSEPH KRASNANSKY

EDITORIAL BOARD

LAURIE ADAMS, Ph.D.
ROBERT BARRY, Ph.D.
POLLY CONDIT, M.S.W.
LLOYD deMAUSE, M.A.
JUDITH R. FELTON, Ph.D.
JOSEPH FLANAGAN, M.S.W.
RICHARD HARRISON, Ph.D.
ROBERT LANE, Ph.D.
SANDA LEWIS, M.S.W.
ELLEN REICH, M.S.W.
PETER D. RICHMAN, Ph.D.
DOROTHY ROSEN, M.A.

JEROME ROSEN
NORMAN SHELLY
ANGELO SMALDINO, M.S.W. J.D.
TERRY SMOLAR, D.S.W.
SIMONE STERNBERG, Ed.D.
ROBERT STORCH, M.S.W.
RONALD SUNSHINE, M.S.W.
RICHARD SYMONS, Ph.D.
MARGOT TALLMER, Ph.D.
GISELA TAUBER, M.S.W., J.D.
ELIZABETH REBECCA TAYLOR, Ed.D.
DONALD WHIPPLE, Ph.D.

Psychoanalytic Approaches With the Hostile and Violent Patient

A LETTER FROM THE EDITOR

Dear Colleague:

Welcome to the second issue of *Current Issues in Psychoanalytic Practice!* We have been heartened by the support and praise from so many of you and have welcomed the constructive criticisms from some of you. We will keep working to bring you what is au courant in psychoanalysis and do it in a way that will be both stimulating and instructive.

We have selected the topic, "Violence and Hostility" for this issue because we feel it is most timely. Our society is being viewed more and more as a hate culture. Competition seems to be valued more than cooperation. People find it easier to disparage and to villify than to love and to support. Childhood murder and adolescent murder are at an all time high. More and more adults are considering violence and hatred as a means of coping with frustration. At the time of this writing, James D. Autry, a convicted murderer, is being taken from death row while outside of the prison, a crowd of people shout for his death and when television lights are turned on Autry, the people chant, "Kill him, kill him!"

When our hate culture sanctions murder and violence, therapists are going to meet sadism, destructive aggression and death wishes in all its forms. This requires constant examination of our countertransference reactions, as Dr. Stanley Rosenblatt's and Dr. Robert Mollinger's articles in this issue so nicely describe. It also necessitates as keen an understanding as possible of patients as do the papers by Dr. Reuben Fine and Dr. Robert Lane suggest. In addition, violence in our society should activate our human empathy as Lucy Freeman's essay denotes. Violence and hostility are complex phenomena and need to be studied in depth and breadth, as the article of Dr. Kutash implies.

© 1984 by The Haworth Press, Inc. All rights reserved.

1

As psychoanalysts and therapists we want to help our patients understand their irrational hatred and destructive aggression so that they can emerge as more loving, more assertive, and more constructive human beings. We trust that this issue will help all of us move with a little more confidence in that direction.

I look forward to chatting with you again in Vol. 1, No. 3. In that issue, we will be talking about approaches to the patient with sexual conflicts.

All of the best,

Herbert S. Strean
Editor

From Hostility to Violence: Some Clinical Observations

Reuben Fine

Every analyst is accustomed to threats of violence, either against him/her or against others. In fact, the amount of violence talked about by patients is staggering. Yet equally staggering is the fact that they almost never carry it out. It would consequently be useful to see under what circumstances the controls are loosened and the threats do become reality. When, in other words, does hostility turn to violence?

Before going to any theoretical explanation, it would be helpful to enumerate a number of cases in which violence did occur, either in the office or outside. Since these would all be occasions in which the usual controls are broken through, they would provide insights about normal repression.

1. Roberta, an attractive young woman of nineteen, was referred for help to a fairly young male psychiatrist. She had poliomyelitis as a child, which led to a prolonged hospitalization of four years, and a residual of a club foot. Partly because of the physical disability, although she was a very sexual girl, she never had a date in her life.

When she arrived at the psychiatrist's office she flew into an uncontrollable rage. Without rhyme or reason she began to throw things around, tried to break a chair, screamed, and acted wild in other ways. The doctor could not control her.

Once in Bellevue, she calmed down immediately and was released very quickly. She then turned to a woman analyst for help. With the woman none of the wild behavior was released. Quite the contrary. She was the docile little girl with mother, quiet, submissive, never disrupting the procedure. With the female analyst she stayed in treat-

© 1984 by The Haworth Press, Inc. All rights reserved.

ment for many years, eventually reaching a reasonable resolution of her life problems.

2. Joseph was also nineteen, the second of two children of well-educated prosperous parents. The older child, his sister, had married and moved out of the house, leaving Joseph the only child at home.

Both parents had very serious problems. For reasons which were hard to fathom, the father was constantly in debt. Although he had a regular civil service job, lived in a modest house in the suburbs, and had no visible vices such as gambling or women which could drain him of money, he never managed to be free of money problems.

The mother also worked at a regular job. She was obviously the boss of the family, who dominated everything. In her background there was no obvious disturbance, but she blamed everybody else for her troubles. She did have one schizophrenic brother, who had been hospitalized since he was thirteen. In the course of time it appeared that she identified her son with this schizophrenic brother.

Originally, the couple came for marital counseling because of their constant quarreling. Much of this seemed trivial in the extreme. He was sixty-two years old, and his parents, in their eighties, were still alive. It was his habit to go to his parents' home for the traditional Friday evening meal; his wife had for twenty years refused to go with him. At the first session, when both were seen by the therapist, she said to him, ''You have to have therapy but it won't do you any good.''

The couple had physical fights, usually with the wife the more aggressive one. He was highly masochistic. Once he came in with a big scratch on his face, reporting, ''Look what I made my wife do to me.'' She had scratched his face with her nails and convinced him that it was his fault.

In this atmosphere it was obvious that Joseph could not grow up too well. He had managed to get away to college. While there he engaged in some homosexual play, but could not relate to girls. After a while the pressure was so great that he returned home, where he transferred to one of the local colleges.

At home, however, he was unable to get along with his parents. Family therapy was tried, to little avail. The mother in particular would fly into such severe frenzies that she would hit him unmercifully; once she actually broke his knee. When she was in a certain state of mind, it became impossible to please her. Thus he eventually learned to apologize to her, but then she would say he did not do it in the right tone of voice.

Her anger even spilled over into the therapy. When her son disobeyed her, she would cancel one of the two sessions scheduled. It was only when the therapist threatened to stop the therapy that she refrained from doing so.

At one point near the beginning of a new college semester he asked his parents for the tuition. They were angry at him, and refused to give him any money. When he came in for his session that day, he demanded that the therapist advance the money for him. When the therapist refused, he became violent and broke an ash tray on the table near the couch. When he saw what he had done, he apologized and eventually paid for the damage.

The case however did not turn out well. Eventually he left treatment with very little resolved. He remained terribly obese, unable to relate to girls, and an overt homosexual.

3. Paul, a thirty-year old physician, was the last one you would expect to display any violence. On the surface, he was very successful; an analytic candidate at one of the local institutes, a flourishing practice, and a charming wife and child. But his background was an extremely traumatic one. Brought up in extreme poverty, he had been a communist throughout his youth. There were six children in his family and all were at odds with one another.

While in medical school, he had married a nurse who adored him. Once out of school, he became more and more dissatisfied with her, particularly with what he saw as her passivity. She was in fact loving and submissive, not really passive, but he could not see it that way.

In the course of his analysis, he became increasingly furious at her and what he insisted was her passivity. Because he had become a poor sleeper, the couple slept in twin beds. One night he became so enraged that he got out of bed and beat her up with his fists.

Eventually, the marriage ended in divorce. Paul did not do well. He became involved in bizarre theories about psychoanalysis, such as the notion that actually carrying out incest cures everything, and began acting out with his patients. Eventually, he died a suicide at an early age.

4. In the case of Philip, the violent incident dated from his childhood. He was one of seven children. When he was nine and his sister two, he was playing with her one day, swinging her between

his legs. His mother yelled at him to stop, busy peeling potatoes. He refused, whereupon she threw the potato peeler at him. His hand was badly cut and he began to bleed profusely. The mother became alarmed at what she had done, and wanted to rush him off to the hospital. He agreed to go only on one condition, that she tell them it was an accident.

In later life Philip became a very masochistic individual, full of anxieties and sexual fears. For a while he worked as an attendant at a mental hospital, where he identified strongly with the patients, although he was never actually hospitalized.

5. Lloyd was a laborer who was drafted into the Navy during World War II. He was a meek, retiring man, who never had much to say. Married, the father of several children, he was generally very reticent and unobtrusive.

In the Navy he did his duty, as ordered. Never in his life had he been in trouble of any kind. While he served on an aircraft carrier which saw some action, that did not seem to bother him; again he did his duty as ordered.

One day, as he was standing in line for his food, another sailor slipped in front of him instead of waiting his turn, and tried to get his food. Lloyd was so incensed at this that he threw the plate in his hand at the other fellow, hitting him full in the face.

After this incident, which was patched up without further complications, Lloyd resumed his old ways. Eventually he was mustered out and went back to his old job. Here he developed a severe bronchial condition (bronchiectasis) which prevented him from working. He was reduced to spending his time at home, watching TV, on a set he had been lucky enough to win in a church raffle.

The V.A. doctors felt that his bronchial condition had a psychic component and referred him for therapy. Here he was almost totally unable to talk, so that therapy did little good. The plate-throwing incident was completely different from anything he had ever done before or since.

6. Sally, a woman in her late thirties (her case has been described in more detail as "Sally the Promiscuous Woman" in my book *The Intimate Hour*) was always in a rage. Her prime symptom was uncontrollable promiscuity, which had been going on for ten years. But she also had outbursts of intense anger, e.g., when she went into a store to buy something and it was not available, or there was something wrong with it, she would scream at the clerk for ten minutes. Actual violence however had never occurred.

Paradoxically, the feeling that brought her to therapy was that she had fallen in love. Her motto in life had always been, "Look ma, no hands," and when she felt some attachment to this new man she became panicky.

Sally's childhood was highly traumatic. The parents had been divorced when she was about four or five; she had one brother and one sister but was close to neither. Her mother had remarried twice, and was still dating heavily in her sixties, after her third divorce (this was less usual thirty years ago, when this patient was seen, than it is today). Sally described her mother as a "cold fish who had no use for anybody." Her mother's philosophy about men was, quite consciously, "Take them for whatever you can get."

Sally's husband knew about her promiscuity, but put up with it because he did the same. When she was away in the Catskills or Florida, he ran around too. Although each knew what the other was doing, the matter was never discussed.

There was one child, a little boy, who naturally was left alone a great deal.

Extreme rage entered the picture from two directions. The first was a suicide attempt by Sally in the course of therapy. This was precipitated by a scene with her lover. They were having a social evening in an apartment with two other couples when the lover suddenly asked her to go into the bedroom; the implication was clear that they would have sex. She did as he wished. But when she got home that evening she took an overdose of pills. Fortunately, she recovered uneventfully although, characteristically, she would not even call the doctor and did not alert the analyst until her next regular session.

The other rage outburst came some years after she had finished therapy. She had had another child, which led her to stop therapy. (When she returned for more therapy ten years later, this incident came out). With her older son there was constant fighting. One day when he disobeyed her, she hit him so hard that she knocked out one of his teeth. Rather than feel sorry for what she had done, she boasted how powerful she was.

Eventually, Sally settled down to a more comfortable life. When she finished the first therapeutic experience, she was reasonably content, though dissatisfied with her husband. He died at an early age of a heart attack. In a subsequent marriage, she experienced strong love feelings which made her very happy.

7. Robert was a thirty-year old teacher who had lost four signifi-

cant adults before he was six years old. When he reached puberty, he developed a symptom of excessive urination. Unfortunately, there was a urologist in the family who advised surgery to widen the urethral opening. The psychological effects of this surgery, especially as performed by a father-figure, were ignored.

In college Robert felt lost. The family arranged for a classical analysis five days a week, which he pursued for some five years. He was always negative about the analyst, released much anger at him, and felt he got little or nothing out of the whole experience.

Once out of college, he began to drift, not knowing where to turn in life. Sexual problems came to the surface. The woman he was seeing urged him to try analysis again.

In the second analysis he did much better. The transference was strongly positive from the very beginning. He felt himself growing, had all kinds of insights into his life and was quite satisfied with himself as a man. However, one major problem gnawed at him; he wanted to be an artist but could not make the grade. Nobody would buy his paintings. He studied for years, with no success.

At one point group therapy was added to the regular individual therapy. In this group there was another man who had wanted to become an artist in his youth, but had also failed to make the grade. The bitterness between these two became extreme.

One day they were arguing about Robert's artistic work. The other group member suggested that perhaps he did not have what it takes. Furious, Robert threw a cup of coffee at him, without doing any real harm.

In this case the outburst proved to be therapeutically fruitful, in that he could see what had set him off and what was holding him back both in his work and in his life.

8. Harry was a twenty-year old salesman of pharmaceutical products. He was always anxious about his business, and one of his resistances took the form of trying to sell the products to his analyst. When, naturally, this was refused, it made him furious.

Harry was the younger of two brothers, and a large part of his associations dealt with his rage at his brother. The brother was three years older, bigger, stronger, had married young and achieved more success in business. Further, the brother had two children, of whom Harry was quite fond. But the jealousy was so intense that he could hardly talk of anything else, even to the extent of arguing that he could be a much better father than his brother, and that he should be permitted to take care of the children.

In addition to a deprived family background, Harry had a horrible history of bad therapy. His first therapist, a woman, embraced him during the first session and then when he wanted to touch her breasts she told him that was not allowed. Another therapist hospitalized him, where he was on thorazine for several months for no good reason. With several other therapists, he could make little contact. One therapist told Harry that he, the therapist, was an overt homosexual; Harry asked whether he felt attracted to him, and the therapist replied that if Harry were not his patient he would be. After Harry left him, the therapist made active overtures to him, even writing him a letter saying that some men just could not make it with women, and Harry should give up the attempt, settling down to a homosexual life.

In the therapy with which I was familiar, Harry took a belligerent attitude. One of his first resistances was to demand that the therapist buy his pharmaceuticals, since he was a doctor. The refusal to do so of course annoyed him, although he was reasonable enough to realize that the request was entirely out of place.

After a while Harry entered most sessions in a boiling fury. One of his favorite actions was to take the box of napkins, which were on the table next to the couch, and threaten to throw them at the analyst. Once he did so, though he made sure to aim so far away that the analyst was not hit. But a number of times he threw the box toward another part of the room. When told he would have to pay for any damage, he agreed, though very little damage ever was done, little more than a few napkins lost.

Eventually, his resistance reached a point where he decided that the analyst could not help him because he was too old. He was then referred to a young therapist, where, as might have been anticipated, he complained that the therapist was too young.

With the new therapist, a similar pattern emerged: picking up objects, threatening to throw them. The climax came once when he actually lifted the couch from the floor, and said he was going to throw it. At this the therapist stopped the session, and warned him that any violence would immediately put an end to the therapy. Harry then calmed down, and eventually wound up with a good analytic result.

9. John was a twenty-two year old young man with a female therapist. He had broken off from his family to such an extent that he lived in a furnished room, and would not allow them to know where he was nor to communicate with him in any way. He went to school and worked at a menial job to support himself and pay the low therapy fee.

Understandably, his transference to the therapist was extremely strong. He worshipped her, wanted to be with her all the time, followed her around. There was no one else in his life. This presents a situation I have described elsewhere (the analytic triad) in which the absence of an outside person intensifies the transference immeasurably.

As usual in such a strong erotic transference, John would fly into terrible rages. The therapist was no good, she did not really love him, she was not treating him right, he should have a better therapist, he was going to complain to the director of the clinic, (which he actually did several times), and so on.

On many occasions John would spend much of his session screaming at his therapist. It became so bad at times that other therapists who were nearby in the clinic would listen to make sure that he was not doing anything to harm her.

Finally, one day he could no longer control himself, and pushed her rather gently on the shoulder. After this he was on the one hand relieved and on the other full of remorse about what he had done. The incident was handled therapeutically and turned out to be very fruitful for the total course of the analysis which in the long run worked out quite well.

10. Hope was a nineteen-year old young woman when she entered therapy. On entering the consulting room she immediately asked the therapist, "Are you married?" When he handled this analytically, she came a few sessions, and then left to get married. Six months later she began to have homosexual dreams, which frightened her, whereupon she really entered therapy.

Once in therapy, she developed a very strong positive transference. She divorced her husband, who was antitherapeutic, and began to date other men. At one point, the therapist noted that she had not gone out for quite a while. When this was pointed out to her she replied, "Of course, we have an agreement. I won't go out with any other men, and you won't go out with any other women." This in spite of the fact that the therapist's office was in his apartment, where his wife was often visible.

Hope was a depressed, anxious young woman. When she graduated from high school, her father told her, "From now on it's down hill." He was opposed to letting her go to college even though she was very bright and had won a scholarship; girls shouldn't go to college. Her mother was equally pessimistic and demeaning. At one point in the analysis, the mother wrote the analyst a letter telling him that he was a quack, that he should tell Hope to give up her job (she was living in New York supporting herself satisfactorily; her mother lived in New Jersey, her father was dead by then), and she went home to her mother, who would take care of her. Her mother insisted that Hope was mentally ill.

After some time, Hope was placed in a group, in combination with individual therapy. In the group some of her more extreme behavior came out, which had been suppressed in the individual sessions; several times she would burst out in long piercing shrieks, just to call attention to her predicament.

The group was composed of five men and five women. Hope became friendly with one of the women, about the same age, Lois, who was married, with two children. Lois' marriage was extremely unhappy and she constantly dreamed of extramarital affairs; several she acted out. Lois and Hope would often fantasize together about being barmaids in a cocktail lounge, which would permit them to pick up men and have sex with them.

After a while, however, Lois began to have an affair with one of the men in the group, actually the oldest member of the group, a father of three children. Occasionally, they would have sex right before the group meeting; once they even went into another room during the group session and had sex on the spot. (The therapist was following a policy that many group therapists adopt of not interfering with any of the activities of the group members unless they became destructive.)

The affair made Hope furiously jealous, as might have been anticipated. Why did he choose Lois rather than her, she was quite willing. One day she became so angry that she picked up a rather heavy ashtray and threw it as hard as she could at Lois, who was sitting across the room. Fortunately, Hope missed Lois; had she hit her, Lois might have been seriously hurt, perhaps even killed. The throw was so strong that a dent was made in the wall.

At this the therapist felt that he had to intervene, so he asked Hope to leave the group but continue with her individual sessions. Reluctantly she agreed, though she could not really understand why she had to be the one to leave rather than Lois.

Eventually, Hope managed to calm down sufficiently to reach an adequate result in the therapy.

11. Barbara, a twenty-year old college student, was in a state of constant depression. For the first year and a half of her analysis she cried every session. She was a lonely, unhappy girl, distant from her family, with few friends.

In the course of her treatment Barbara succeeded in attracting a number of men, largely by agreeing to have sex with them. After the sex went on for a while they would generally drop her. Upon graduation from college, she took a job as a clerical worker, a job which called for almost no skills other than filing and typing.

The transference was very negative. She accused the analyst of being a capitalist, of gouging his patients out of their money, of caring nothing about her.

At one point she said: "You can't understand me; you've succeeded at everything you've ever done, while I've failed at everything."

Eventually, she met a man who seemed to care very much for her. As usual, she allowed herself to be completely dominated by him, but unlike the others he did not take advantage of her submissiveness. He was a member of a small left-wing group which engaged in violent demonstrations, at times attacking the police directly, which would lead to arrest. Once he was sent to jail and raped homosexually.

Barbara had no strong convictions about his left-wing sympathies, but since he was her man now, she went along with him. He suffered from premature ejaculation when he first met her, and accepted a referral for therapy. The prematurity cleared up very quickly and he left treatment, remaining an avowed enemy of psychoanalysis even though it had been of considerable help to him. But he was caught up in the notion that psychoanalysis is the last stand of capitalism.

One of his main sources of protest was going to demonstrations where police were present, and engaging in some kind of violence. Barbara herself was not inclined to behave in that way, but she went along with him, although she did not do anything.

One day she came in and announced that she had been arrested because she had kicked a policeman. At first she insisted that the policeman, who was mounted, had attacked her. After a while, however, she revealed that the police had made every effort not to hit anybody. When they refused to be aggressive, she deliberately kicked one policeman in the shin, and was arrested. Because of the nature of the demonstration, and the fact that the policeman had not been hurt, she was released very quickly.

12. Leonard, a twenty-five year old veteran in a mental hospital, was taking a battery of psychological tests. He went along in the usual manner until he reached card 11M of the Thematic Apperception Test. This card has an unpopulated background and is usually

seen as some mountain fastness or simple outdoor scene. It rarely arouses any strong emotions. Leonard, however, as soon as he saw the picture, instead of telling a story about it, as he had been instructed to do, went into a catatonic stupor in which he remained incommunicado for two days.

When he came out of his stupor, and had finished all the tests, the testor asked him whether he would care to explain his behavior in reaction to Card 11; it would be helpful if he could, he was told, but he should not feel any compulsion to do so.

Thereupon, he told the following story: When he was on Okinawa during World War II, he was walking along one day in an isolated spot, and saw two people in the distance, a man and woman. Thinking that they were Japanese, he shot at them, killing the man. When he got closer, he realized that they were Okinawans. The woman, fearful that he would kill her too, offered herself to him sexually. He accepted.

Somehow the card aroused memories of that violent sexual incident, which still elicited strong guilt feelings in him.

The testing was to serve the purpose of a differential diagnosis. It was decided that though very disturbed, he was not yet schizophrenic. Several days later, he approached the chief psychiatrist at the hospital, and asked him to operate to remove the rats from his brain. With the revelation of this overt delusion he was sent to a custodial hospital. I have no record of what happened to him afterwards.

Paul Federn used to warn his students that schizophrenics were extremely vulnerable, and that even a Rorschach test might precipitate an overt psychosis. This may be one of the kinds of cases he was talking about.

13. A number of cases can be included here in which the patient (or family member) felt no guilt whatsoever about either threatened or actual violence.

Donald, a sixty-five year old man who had never married, was understandably full of violent thoughts. He would punch this man in the jaw, knock that man down, get even with that one. He even boasted that he had Mafia connections, and that if pushed hard enough he would resort to them.

One of his self-destructive patterns was to become involved with very young women, some of them prostitutes. When the self-damaging nature of these activities was pointed out to him, his invariable reply was, "What's wrong with young women?" or, "What's wrong with prostitutes?"

On one occasion he picked up a girl at a coffee shop, and took her home for sex. It turned out that she was a prostitute, working in a massage parlor. He became enamored of her, and tried to see her on a regular basis. She showed no interest in him, not even when offered money, preferring to stay in her massage parlor and receive him there. But she did apparently tease him, saying that she would meet him at a certain place, then never showing up.

After a while he became so angry that the analytic hours were filled with schemes to kill her. He would get the Mafia after her, he would cut her throat, he would beat her to death. Nothing of all this materialized, and after a while he managed to forget about her.

Belle, a very sick thirty-year old woman, came to treatment to get away from her boy friend, who was a detective, and wanted to marry her. She had had four children: two had been given away at birth, the other two were taken away from her by court order. The boy friend had the totally unrealistic wish to marry her and have a child with her. Whenever she protested he would beat her up physically. She wished to have some therapy, rather than stay in this mess, but was helpless against his physical beatings. One could of course surmise that this was a classical sado-masochistic pair, but the main point stressed here is that he felt no guilt about his violence.

June, an attractive young woman in her twenties, began dating a man who seemed suitable in many ways. But one day he revealed that he always carried a knife in his boots, which were ankle-length, so that the knife could be concealed. He urged her to carry a knife too, so that she would not have to be afraid of muggers. Since he was in therapy, both individual and group, she suggested that he take this up in therapy, and get rid of the knife. To her surprise he told her that the therapist himself had suggested it to him, and that the group was fully behind him in his attitudes. She discontinued the relationship.

DISCUSSION

The initial question which it was hoped the clinical material would help to answer was: How is it that patients express such enormous amounts of hostility on the couch, yet are rarely violent in real life? As the cases are reviewed, it turns out this is the most common pattern encountered. In no fewer than eight of the cases (Joseph, Philip, Lloyd, Robert, Harry, John, Barbara and Leonard) this pattern was clear.

In all of the cases there was an underlying sense of despair. Life held little hope for them, and a number actually turned out badly. Joseph became very obese and a homosexual; Leonard relapsed into a schizophrenic state, Lloyd retreated from life completely. The act of violence, which was brought out in the therapy (in one case, acted out in the therapist's office), was related to the despair. Just why the violence should be set off in the situations in which it was is not easily clarified. Perhaps the most plausible explanation is that each one said at some point: Thus far and no further.

Yet after the outburst they generally relapsed into their previous state. Thus the entire pattern must be examined, not just the act of violence. In their inner despair they try one resolution or another, which does not work out. Finally, they cannot stand it any longer, and strike out. After that they relapse into their old state all over again or, as with Leonard, into something worse.

I am reminded of a patient I once saw on a ward of lobotomized veterans. He would walk up and down the center of the room for hours at a stretch. When he got to a certain point, somewhere in the middle, he would punch out with his right arm. If someone happened to be there he would hit him; if not, he would simply punch into the air.

The despair of the patients described in this paper, as well as the lobotomized veterans, related to their total life situation. They saw no way out. Barbara (as noted) cried in every session for the first year and a half of her therapy. What is of most importance, as mentioned, is not to separate the violence from the rest of their lives. What is of more importance than the violence itself is the constant feeling of inadequacy and meaninglessness of life which they experience.

Three of the cases connect the violence with frustrated sexuality. The case of Roberta is particularly revealing: she broke out into a terrible destructive rage when she got close to a man, but with a woman she was able to manage. Genetically, this could be seen as part of the switch from mother to father, which the child goes through in the course of its entire development, not merely at the Oedipal level. Just why Roberta should vent her spleen on a man, while Hope would do so on a woman, derives from the differing nature of their childhood backgrounds.

But here too the underlying sexual frustration is the most important element. That Sally led a completely promiscuous sex life for ten years does not reduce the terrible frustration she felt in her life;

it again shows that sex without love may be temporarily gratifying, but in the long run it leads to resentment and hopelessness. Sally's suicide attempt was a good example of her deep feeling of hopelessness, which she was otherwise able to cover up.

The case of Paul illustrates the theme of aggression (in this case not violence) followed by suicide. There was a wild acting out; at one point he began to have sex with all the patients who would agree to do so, both men and women. His goal, he said, was to "break through" the incest barrier; only if this could be done would the patients be helped.

Finally, there are the instances where there is no guilt about the violence. Here too, looked at more carefully, the persons involved were extremely disturbed, and the acting out of their violence, either in reality or in fantasy, did not reduce their inner conflicts to any appreciable degree.

There are many theories of hostility; since this is a clinical paper, I shall not review them in detail. The reader who is interested in the historical development may consult my *History of Psychoanalysis* (1979). These cases bring out one vital point: whether the hostility is acted out or repressed, the person remains in terrible turmoil. Some therapists really believe that the "cure" of repressed hostility is to encourage the patients to act out; thus a patient of mine once told me of a group of which she had heard in which each participant was provided with a wet sponge, and whenever he or she felt the urge, they would throw it at some other group member. This is a theoretical confusion based on some misconceived notion of catharsis. Violence is not a catharsis, it is a cover-up for deeper conflicts.

SUMMARY

The question raised is this: Since there is much anger brought out in the analytic situation, how is it that so little of it spills over into actual violence? To answer this question, a number of cases are reviewed, both patients in therapy and others. It was found that in most cases the violent outbursts sprang from a deep sense of inner despair; the violence was just an incident. Of far greater consequence is the sense of meaninglessness, depression, aimlessness and confusion which lies at the root of these people's lives. In many cases the analytic process holds back the violence, which would otherwise be acted out, and allows the person to work out the inner conflicts and reach a more reasonable resolution of life's conflicts. This, I would suggest, is the major reason why we see so much hostility in analysis and so little violence. It is not so much that violence is repressed, though that does happen. More important is the fact that the consistent analysis of the underlying despair reduces the need for the violence.

The "Seeds" of Murder as Sown "in the Nursery"

Lucy Freeman

The genius that was Freud has been attested to no more brilliantly or eloquently than Flora Rheta Schreiber has done in *The Shoemaker,* a book that is bound to become a classic. She shows in dramatic form exactly what Freud predicted would happen if the aggressive and erotic drives were not fused but remained separate, in their primitive states, because of lack of love and tenderness during childhood to soften the raw fury of the hostile urges.

Freud also said the "seeds" of wholesale murder—war—were sown in the nursery and *The Shoemaker* is proof of this truth. The book is strong and shocking, the ugly stuff of the id unleashed—cannibalistic, vengeful, murderous—when a child is the victim of severe physical and psychological abuse.

Professor Schreiber (she teaches at the John Jay College of Criminal Justice) gives us a blow by blow (literally) portrait of the very early and the subsequent tragedies that were the seeds of Joseph Kallinger's desire, first to save the world, and then destroy it, as his adoptive parents had first saved him from a life at the orphanage and then psychologically destroyed him. His final fantasy, the one that brought him down, was to kill every human being, but not just kill— kill through the destruction of sexual organs as he felt his sexual organs had been destroyed by brutal parents. The actual targets, as they seldom are, were not the ones on whom Kallinger wreaked his revenge as he indulged in a series of burglaries, an attempted rape and three murders. The innocent, unfortunately, were the victims of a consuming fear and hatred that could no longer be contained.

To accomplish the herculean task of persuading a murderer to expose his tormenting memories requires an extraordinarily sympathetic and sensitive person. Professor Schreiber, author of *Sybil,* in which she helped uncover the hidden layers of a young woman with

© 1984 by The Haworth Press, Inc. All rights reserved. *19*

sixteen personalities, showed she possessed the rare ability to inspire trust and to provide the empathy that would permit a deeply troubled man to reveal his crippled soul, to cut through the denials we all summon to preserve our sanity. And in *The Shoemaker,* Professor Schreiber found a man willing to contribute what he could out of the dark and bloody past so others might benefit from the knowledge the book would convey.

To get personal for a moment, I know how difficult it is to try to persuade a convicted murderer to bare his soul. I tried, while living in Chicago in 1953, to persuade William Heirens to tell me about his emotional life. Reporters called him "the lipstick killer," for he wrote in lipstick on the mirror of the bureau of one woman victim, "Catch me before I kill more."

The day I met my first and only murderer, the fact that he was safely behind bars was little comfort. I was still afraid. Not only because he hated females—he was convicted of murdering two women and a six-year old girl—but because I was fearful of delving into the dark terrors that had driven him to murder when he was only seventeen and completing his freshman year at the University of Chicago. Terrors, I was sure, he did not understand or was able to deal with, and terrors I possessed which I had not as yet dealt with in my psychoanalysis.

The warden at Stateville Penitentiary in Joliet, where Heirens had served eight years of three consecutive life sentences, introduced me to Heirens. I had expected a monster to fit the monstrous crimes. Instead, I faced a husky, rather handsome man of twenty-six who looked as though he should be in the fields behind a plough. He stared at me with hazel eyes that showed cool detachment. He agreed to talk and we met many times in the visitors' room, where he spoke of his childhood and later life. He denied committing the crimes, claiming the evidence was obtained while he was under sodium amytol, and not valid. His mother told me somewhat of his early development, including the fact she had started to miscarry when two months pregnant. He had been a difficult baby, refusing to feed at her breast, then throwing up the bottle formula, and, in her words, "I didn't expect him to live." She admitted she rarely fondled him, that she was confused as to how to bring him up. When he was seven months, he toppled out of his carriage down twelve cement steps to the basement (why was he left in such a dangerous spot?) of their small house. When I visited it, I was shocked by the tiny bedroom in which Heirens, for the first few years of his life, had slept in a crib next to his parents' bed. He told me he hoped someday to build his own house and it would have two basements. When I asked why two, he said, "So the pumping won't keep me awake all night."

I hoped the book, *Before I Kill More,* showed some connection between Heirens' childhood fantasies and his experiences with his mother and father, and the later murders. As the late Dr. Dexter Bullard, director of Chestnut Lodge, once said to me, "You didn't have enough psychological evidence but you reached the right conclusions." A grudging compliment but I welcomed it.

Then Truman Capote's *In Cold Blood* went far deeper into lives of two murderers in Kansas, showing how their childhoods had been devoid of love and protection, arousing intense aggression. And now Professor Schreiber gives us as full a picture as it seems humanly possible to provide of why men are driven to murder. True, she describes only one man, his unique fantasies and experiences. But the emotions that moulded his crimes are shared by all of us. Most of us are able to control our murderous rage because we received a fair amount of love and protection from parents. But the book offers a look into our own hearts and the natural need for vengeance we feel when we are hurt, physically or psychologically, when we feel rejected and alone in a world composed only of enemies.

Joseph Kallinger, a thirty-eight year old Philadelphia shoemaker, along with his son Michael, thirteen, were arrested on January 17, 1975 for breaking into five suburban homes in Pennsylvania, Maryland and New Jersey. During the Leonia, New Jersey break-in, Kallinger held eight people hostage and murdered a young nurse.

Professor Schreiber met him for the first time on July 19, 1976 as he was in Bergen County Jail awaiting trial for murder. After a few interviews with him, she realized he was "drifting in and out of contact with reality." He knew it too and, frightened, wrote her at New York City's John Jay College of Criminal Justice, where she is Professor of English and Speech: "Please come to help me here at Camden County Jail. I need help to find my self and I only feel comfortable when talking to you face to face. . .I trust you, and I always feel better after our talks. . .The trust is important to me. And I must know the truth or life is not worth living."

Professor Schreiber writes in the book:

He fascinated me. He was verbal and analytical, charming, intelligent and poetic. Extraordinarily sensitive, he was also a murderer who couldn't tell the difference between his visions and reality, between the phantoms that haunted him and the people who he thought were trying to destroy him. He was full of paradoxes.

Though the book deals with crime, essentially it is "an exploration of madness," she says. "It is the first inside—that is, internal— look at a psychotic killer: a man whose psychosis drives him to kill." She describes a "psychotic killer" as "very different from a psychopathic killer who murders for money or the pleasure of killing." Kallinger is delusional, paranoid, obviously psychotic. But we might ask if all killers, no matter what the conscious motive, are not mad to a certain degree. Who but a madman would kill an innocent fellow human being? If you believe this, it has ramifications far beyond what society, at this point, is willing to provide in the way of rehabilitation for murderers, whether obviously psychotic like Kallinger or psychopathic, like the murderers of *In Cold Blood.*

Kallinger said to Professor Schreiber one hot night in August, 1977, as they sat across a small wooden table in the Camden County Jail,

Flora, what makes up a man? How sane am I? Yes, I talk sane at times, but without warning, something else emerges like the shadow but more concealed and deadly. What is the trigger? Find that answer and you got the man and you can start him moving on paper from the friendly neighborhood shoemaker to the living time bomb so deadly concealed that not even the most sophisticated detection device can spot it.

She answered his question. She found the "trigger" and also "what makes up a man," as she spent more than one thousand hours over the next six years interviewing him, first in the State Correctional Institution at Huntingdon, Pennsylvania, and then in Farview State Hospital for the Criminally Insane. He was committed to Farview because he had gone on a hunger strike and the prison did not have the means to break it. After eighteen days, prison authorities sent him to Farview for forced feeding. Week after week, with the unrelenting persistence of the gifted investigative reporter, Professor Schreiber slowly helped Kallinger unveil the severe psychological and physical damage he suffered as a child, as well as recalling two additional murders he had buried from consciousness, one his own son, the other a ten-year old Puerto Rican boy.

Both Professor Schreiber and Joseph Kallinger deserve praise for this epic honesty. He hid nothing once she gained his trust. The book took tremendous courage on both their parts. It is not easy for a lone woman to be in the company of a murderer, even though protected by guards, and it could not have been easy for Kallinger to reveal the agony and anguish within. It is never easy to reveal agony or anguish, even after many years on the couch in the presence of a trained psychoanalyst.

Consider these facts and the fantasies they must have aroused in the life of the terrified infant and child that was Kallinger: an illegitimate love-child, breast-fed for a week while in a Philadelphia hospital with his mother after his birth, then breast-fed for three weeks when she stayed at the house of a friend, afraid to take him to her own home, then placed by his mother in a private boarding home where he remained until he was two months and nine days. Then his mother gave him to St. Vincent's Catholic Orphanage where nurse-nuns, sexually inhibited single women dedicated to serving God, gave institutional care. Kallinger's mother, who had a daughter by a husband from whom she was seeking a divorce, was Jewish. She had fallen in love with a married man, discovered she was pregnant, but he refused to leave his wife—he was Catholic and Italian. She was afraid if she admitted her pregnancy, her husband would not allow her to keep her daughter after the divorce, so she gave up her illegitimate son.

When he was twenty-two months old, he was seen by Anna and Stephen Kallinger, a childless couple seeking a son to adopt. They had visited the Catholic orphanage and decided to take home the dark-haired, handsome baby. The Kallingers were immigrants from Europe who met in Philadelphia. Anna came from the lowlands of Austria, Stephen, from Hungary. He had learned the trade of shoemaker.

It soon becomes clear the Kallingers were psychotic or pre-psychotic. Their sadistic acting out of sexual and hostile fantasies was revealed when the boy was six years and nine months. They took him to St. Mary's Hospital in Philadelphia for a hernia operation, which was to leave a six-inch scar low on his left side. Such an operation in itself is terrifying to a six-year old. After they brought him home, they told him the doctor had "done something else" to him at the hospital—he "fixed your little bird" (their word for penis) and removed "the demon who lived in your little bird," implying he would grow up impotent. Anna told him, "Your bird won't get hard because the demon is gone. Always you will be soft there. So you're gonna be a good boy, a good man. Never get in no trouble. Never get a girl in trouble."

It would be difficult to imagine a more psychologically cruel threat to a little boy. In addition, he received no sign of love or tenderness or respect from these parents. They never gave him a birthday present nor acknowledged the day of his birth—denying he even existed. They would not allow him to play with other children but treated him as a shoemaker's robot who, duly programmed, would be an expert shoemaker. He worked on shoe repair after school and part-time or full-time, if needed, on Saturdays. He was not permitted to go to parties, to roller or ice skate, ride a bicycle, visit the homes of other children or bring them into the red brick row house where he lived.

Once when he was eight, he desperately wanted to go to the zoo with the other children but Anna insisted he stay home and work. For the first time he rebelled, told her, "Dad said I could go to the zoo and I'm going!" Infuriated by his defiance of her order, she reached for a hammer used for driving nails through layers of leather. She hit him on the head four times with the heavy steel instrument, the cuts bled profusely. His father frequently flogged him with homemade cat-o'-nine-tails he made out of leather and rawhide laces, cracking the boy on the back, the arms, the head. The cruelty was thus physical too.

When he was ten, he stole rolls of nickels, dimes and quarters from his parents' bedroom to bribe neighborhood children to go with him to the movies on Saturdays. His parents caught him stealing their money, took him downstairs, turned on the stove burner and put, first the fingers of his right hand, then his left hand, into the flames as Stephen intoned, "This will burn the demon thief out of the fingers that steal." But the boy kept stealing the coins and his parents kept burning his hands—six times more—until finally he gave up the stealing.

It is a severe indictment of our adoptive procedures that the Kallingers' abuse of the youth was never uncovered. Not only violence but sexual abuse was part of his childhood. When he was eight, he was homosexually molested by three older boys in a vacant lot four blocks from his home. He did not dare tell his parents, afraid they would blame him for not coming home at once, since they had sent him out on an errand, the only way he was allowed out of the house. He had wandered into an abandoned lot on which there were old empty oil tanks and the three boys had seized him.

As he grew up, Kallinger slowly edged into a sort of respectability but beneath it lurked the response to the madness that had been inflicted on him. He became a fine shoemaker under his father's tutelage, never struck his parents even when they beat him or burned his fingers. But as he grew bigger the Kallingers became afraid of the youth (afraid he might retaliate for their cruelty) and barricaded themselves in their room at night so he could not enter and perhaps murder them.

When he was fifteen, with their approval, after he fell in love with a girl named Hilda, he moved into a furnished room in a house six blocks away, still working at the Kallinger shop. The Kallingers let him go, no doubt relieved of the fear he would get even. He married Hilda a year later and they had two children. They were divorced after five years, as she called him "crazy" and made fun of his "small penis." Three months after the divorce, he married his present wife, Betty, with whom he had five children.

Over the years he was a good parent, when not beset by fantasies. He became involved far more than his wife in the children's activities in school. But the fantasies grew stronger as he set up a torture chamber in the basement where he disciplined the children, sticking pins into his daughter's naked body, at times beating one or another of his four sons. When he finally burned the thighs of his now-teenage daughter with a hot spatula (as his parents had once burned his hands) after she went out with a boy of whom he disapproved, and beat one son over the head with a hammer, the children had him arrested and he was charged with child abuse. At that time he pleaded for psychiatric help and two psychiatrists and a clinical psychologist recommended he be hospitalized. But the judge sent him home because he was "a good provider" and the children were "better off with him in the house."

Kallinger was now hearing the voices of God and the devil instructing him to kill people. One day he and one son set out bent on murder and they lured the ten-year old Puerto Rican boy, away from a swimming pool under the pretext of hiring him for a few hours' work. They then mutilated him sexually in an abandoned rug factory (as Kallinger had been seduced as a boy in an abandoned oil tank).

Kallinger's delusions grew wilder and wilder and finally he was consumed by a desire to destroy all mankind through the destruction of sexual organs. His oral fury was shown in all its horror when he ordered the nurse in the Leonia house he invaded, to bite off the penis of a young man he had tied up in the cellar. When she refused, saying she would rather die than commit such an unspeakable act, he stabbed her over and over with a hunting knife as he had an erection and ejaculation during the assault. The knife and sex were related; he kept a knife under his pillow when he had intercourse with his wife (perhaps symbolic of the doctor's knife that had invaded his body in the hernia operation, and which, his mother and father told him, in effect, had castrated him).

Kallinger told Professor Schreiber: "My mind, ever since I was twelve, has been full of pictures of cutting sexual organs, both male and female. I used this thinking through the years mostly so I could be potent first with Hilda, then with Betty. But I can see now that it had another purpose: Without the images, which brought me erections, I couldn't obey God's command [to kill]." Here again is the close connection between violence and sex—he had to feel violent and then carry out violence in order to fulfill himself sexually.

The late Dr. Silvano Arieti, a leading authority on schizophrenia, examined Kallinger at Professor Schreiber's request in 1980 and 1981, and described him as suffering from paranoid schizophrenia, characterized by delusions and hallucinations. The roots of his adult schizophrenia lay in his experiences during his first two years of life without a mother or father, but what determined the severity of the illness and the form it took was what was done to him by his adoptive parents, Dr. Arieti said. The specific childhood incident involving castration fantasies, after the hernia operation, was so threatening that, as an adolescent he was clearly delusional about the alleged "castration," Dr. Arieti believed. Kallinger was also delusional when he stabbed photographs of breasts and penises and when, at the age of thirteen, he planned to castrate a boy who was standing beside a creek but then fled from the scene, realizing his life would end in disaster if he committed such an act. But later the fantasy was too strong for him to be able to stop carrying it out.

Dr. Lewis L. Robbins, former director of adult psychiatry at the Menninger Foundation, who later examined Kallinger at Farview, wrote in his report that he concurred with Dr. Arieti's findings that Kallinger

chronically suffers from paranoid schizophrenia and that his criminal behavior is a manifestation of his illness. . . In retrospect it seems evident that had his illness been recognized earlier and treatment instituted when he was arrested for child abuse before he commited any crimes and had he subsequently been committed to a hospital rather than considered sane and hence imprisoned, the course of events might have been less pathological.

It wasn't until Kallinger was sent to Farview that he received any psychological help, after examinations at Farview found him "floridly psychotic." He had been sentenced to serve a thirty-to-eighty year prison sentence, with two other consecutive sentences.

Professor Schreiber managed to locate Kallinger's mother, at his request. His mother consented to go to Farview to see him for the first time since she had given him up as a baby, and he met her when he was forty-two, for the first time in his memory. He had scribbled questions in advance for his mother to answer, including: Why had you left me? Did you think of me through the years? What would you have wanted for me? Did you miss me? Were you sorry after you gave me up? But he never put the questions to her. They talked instead of trivial matters. She told Professor Schreiber there had never been any mental illness or crime in her family.

As they left, Kallinger's mother said, "I expected him to be resentful. But he was extremely polite. I can say one thing for the Kallingers: They reared a very well-mannered man." Then, as the two women looked back and saw Kallinger waving at them, his mother said, "He looks like a little boy." Professor Schreiber commented, "That's what he is, a deserted little boy." She may have been thinking of the time he tried to commit suicide in prison and lay naked in his isolation cell, crying out, "Mama."

If we really want to understand why men murder so we can try to prevent murder, we will recognize the importance of this book beyond its sensational story. While most of the reviews have praised the book highly, some have denigrated Professor Schreiber for "siding" with a murderer, asking how dare she show such sympathy for so villainous a man? She is not condoning Kallinger's acts, she is explaining why he was driven to them. The critics do not understand that her goal was to show the terrifying power of the unconscious part of the mind, they have no concept of the role the unconscious plays in the person who commits murder. They think of the mind as simplistic—good and bad. They want an eye for an eye.

They are incapable of tolerating their own murderous feelings, of being aware of the inner rage in others or themselves that may cause rape and slaughter.

It is slow going, this attempt to help people understand why the aggressive instinct gets so out of control that a man *must* kill, or world wars *must* be waged. The world is so dangerous a place because so many homes are so dangerous for children. That is what Professor Schreiber is saying, as she describes an extreme example which shows up the lesser rage in all of us. We all have been subjected to what Freud called "the human condition"—the long years of childhood, of bondage to a particular mother and father. The atrocities Kallinger committed are at the extreme end of the scale of vengeance. They show the severity of the tortures he endured as a child, tortures most of us are spared.

His ego had little chance to form, deprived as he was, for the first two years of life, of the slightest vestige of a mother's loving care. Then his foster parents, instead of strengthening the vulnerable ego, crippled it beyond repair. It eventually collapsed, prey to the primitive id, as the fury he had been unable to express as a child erupted in bursts of madness. The distorted fantasies that fueled his crimes were "crazy" to the rest of the world but not crazy to the abused child trying to make sense of the depraved brutality shown by a barbaric mother and father—"mentally ill," in kinder words.

As was done to him he later did unto others—in spades, as the saying goes, usually the case. The child often caricatures his parents as he internalizes them, cruelty and all; he dramatizes his woes so the world will know what he had suffered. The world should not forget the suffering of Joseph Kallinger and the suffering he was unconsciously driven to inflict on his children and strangers. In describing his life so openly to Professor Schreiber, he is saying, take a lesson from my torment, try to save other children from such horror if you want to stop their suffering and keep them from murdering the innocent.

If he had received psychological help along the way, three people today would be alive. This is one of the strong messages of this heartbreaking book. Perhaps somewhere Freud is applauding. Ah, but he didn't believe in either heaven or hell. He once wrote a friend that his aim was to help people out of the hell they created on earth. *The Shoemaker* shows what a hell life can be if a child knows no love but only hatred and cruelty.

Terrorizing the Analyst

Sidney M. Rosenblatt

The main theme of this paper is that children who have been systematically terrorized by their parents through the process of identification with the aggressor will develop a transference as patients in therapy and analysis of systematically terrorizing their analyst. In order for the analysis of these patients to proceed, it is necessary that the therapist very quickly recognize this particular type of transference and be able to take measures to deal with it so that the analysis not be sabotaged. As an example of the use of terror, I would like to quote from a historical study of the life of Adolf Hitler called *The Psychopathic God* by the historian Robert G.L. Waite, published by Basic Books in 1977. This study is particularly interesting in that the author, while a historian, has been very meticulous in searching out psychological insights and clues into the life of Hitler.

Very early in Hitler's career, with the publication of *Mein Kampf,* he systematically described how he would use terror as a means of political subjugation. There are of course a great many aspects to the psychopathology and the life of Adolf Hitler, but for the purposes of this paper, I am focusing just on Hitler's need for, interest in, and use of terror and relating it to some possible events in Hitler's childhood.

We know that Hitler is the only surviving child of a father, Alos Schickelbuber, and a mother, Clara Klotzel Hitler. Hitler's father was a minor petty official in the Austrian bureaucracy. There are many instances in the book of Hitler's father being quite authoritarian, using corporal punishment to a large extent and also apparently arousing an enormous amount of terror and fear in the young Adolf in order to insure obedience. Hitler's father evidently could only control a child through the intense and excessive use of terror, so that to a child he became a terrifying father figure. While Hitler's career can be explained by many different causes from a psychoanalytic point of view, from Hitler's use of terror it seems

© 1984 by The Haworth Press, Inc. All rights reserved.

quite clear that through identification with the aggressor he became the terrorizer, terrorizing huge populations and nations as he himself had been terrorized as a child.

According to Waite, Hitler's father was not only intensely sadistic towards his son but also towards Hitler's mother, often beating them both mercilessly. It is interesting to note that Waite mentions that there is a good deal of evidence that Hitler's perversions took the sexual form of needing a younger woman to defecate and urinate on him in order to achieve sexual satisfaction.

The parent who uses terror excessively is someone who generally feels quite bad about himself, has no sense of his own worth, and relies almost entirely on subjecting the child to intimidation through terror. Because of the parent's despair, basically, this is the only way the child can be controlled, for if terror is not used, the child becomes uncontrollable and chaos will ensue.

My own experience as an analyst with patients who have been terrorized as children, and who then develop a very intense terrorizing transference to the analyst, comes mainly from two very interesting patients. One is the last son of a very prominent jurist in a community in upper New York State who, upon entering analysis, informed me that he hoped to become very prominent in a revolutionary organization and hoped that in his lifetime he would see a major social revolution in which he would have enormous power and would become Commissar for the Arts. At that point, he said, he would be able to assert power and control over all artists and, additionally, over his analyst who, although not an artist, would surely not escape the patient's wish for complete power and control once the revolution occurred.

Very quickly in the analysis it became apparent that many threats were used by the patient. Often they would be made in such a ludicrous manner that it was very difficult to believe that the patient was in any way serious. From his opening statements, it appeared that the patient was suffering from a quite severe type of psychopathology, certainly some form of schizophrenia. During the analysis, or rather the psychotherapy interviews, he made threats of suing the therapist, of subpoenaing him for legal action. It was clear that in making these threats the patient was reliving in the analytic session threats that had been repeatedly made to him by his father, the prominent jurist, in order to insure control of his son. However, any attempts to interpret this aspect of transference were of no avail. He was showing a type of psychotic transference in which thinking is not very much influenced by any verbal interpretation the therapist could make. Nevertheless, the patient was able to continue in therapy approximately four times per week for two years and was able to make some gains in his life, achieving more of a stability in an otherwise extremely chaotic and fragmented life.

The second case was a young man who was the son of a shoe salesman in the Bronx. His mother was a medical secretary at a large medical center. This young man also continually made threats about suing the analyst, and continually felt he was unjustly treated. He would often rant and rave, be verbally abusive, and at one point even attempted physical abuse.

This young man was the son of a man who had established some minor degree of financial security for himself and his family. When I saw the patient, his mother and father in a joint interview, the father seemed like a small, assuming, unimposing man, but in his relationship with his son as a child, he used terror as a main means of child discipline. And from that, the child, as he grew up, developed a need to use terror towards others through identification with the aggressor.

Another patient was the youngest daughter of a cook in a restaurant, who had been continually threatened throughout her life by her mother with being sent away to an orphanage, or being hospitalized for mental illness. She had been continually beaten as a child. In her analysis, which has now gone on for ten years, she started off by using threats of suing the analyst and often made attempts to be physically violent towards the analyst after threatening violence. Through analyzing her systematic terrorization as a child, during the past ten years, the analyst helped her give up much of her terrorizing tactics, and her relationships with others in her therapy group, with her analyst, and with people in general have improved significantly.

Had the analyst not recognized the use of terror as a systematic ploy in the patient's armamentation and her need to deal with this, both in its transference and countertransferential effects, the patient's therapy would not have gone as well.

In considering both the countertransference and transference implications of the patient terrorizing the analyst, it is clear that although the motivation of the patient for terrorizing the analyst has to do with the patient's early infantile conflicts and learning, since terrorizing is a two-way street, the analyst has some need to be terrorized by the patient. This is due to his earlier sadistic and masochistic fantasies and interactions between him and his early caretakers.

With the patient who has been terrorized as a child, the analyst may fall into the trap of becoming the victim of the patient because of the analyst's own feelings of victimization by his parents or other caretaking figures. Very intense sadistic and masochistic fantasies are quickly mobilized in the analyst as a result of interacting with the terrorizing patient. These fantasies can become of such overwhelming proportions that they interfere with the analyst's ability to understand the situation, to be aware of it, and to deal with it analytically.

Often the intense anxiety aroused in the analyst by the terrorizing patient leads either to a complete capitulation with intense sadistic and masochistic fantasies on the analyst's part as he gives in to the terror tactics of the patient, or becomes intensely rigid and immediately tries to establish rules and boundaries in such a way that the patient is terrified, overwhelmed and usually leaves therapy.

It is only through the analyst's understanding and analysis of his own intense sado-masochistic needs evoked in the terrorizing situation, that the possibility of a viable analytic relationship can be formed. Usually patients who have intense needs to terrorize an analyst will only stay if they sense that there is some possibility in the analyst that he can indeed be terrorized.

Most of us as analysts, and as people, have at some time in our lives been terrorized by our parents and subject to intense sadistic and masochistic maneuvers where we have either become the victim of our parents or the terrorizer of our parents. In numerous ways, depending upon our own individual histories, the possibilities for a very intense sadistic and masochistic relationship between the patient and the therapist/analyst very quickly comes to the fore. It is only through understanding and analyzing our own sadistic and masochistic needs and fantasies, which often may be unconscious, as they come out through our dreams about the patient, that we have some possibility of being helpful to a patient. Otherwise, the tendency to act out with the patient our very intense sadistic or masochistic fantasies becomes overwhelming.

In our own times the fear and fascination of terrorism is endemic, having to do with the intense sadistic and masochistic culture in which we are living. Since there is the great possibility that civilization as we know it can be destroyed, literally at the push of a button, we are left with an enormous amount of unresolved anxiety. Often this is taken out on children, colleagues, patients, and patients of course take it out on therapists. Along with the current terror, very intense sadistic and masochistic fantasies are also endemic. It is only through our attempt to understand this and to work with it in an analytic fashion that we can at least get off the wheel of being alternately victim and terrorizer of ourselves, our patients and our families.

Self Defense:
Multiple Personality
and the Fear of Murder

Robert N. Mollinger

The *Oxford English Dictionary* defines "self" as "that which in a person is really and intrinsically *he*" and "a permanent subject of successive and varying states of consciousness." Intrinsic, the self is essential; permanent, it is fixed and unchanging; a subject, it is grammatically, a doer of actions and, philosophically, the mind or what thinks. In a sense, the "self" is the "I", as in "I exist," "I think," and "I fear."

Psychoanalytically, self can be examined as the whole person including his psyche and body or as a specific mental construct. In the second, specific sense, the self can best be understood in terms of "mental self-representations," that is, the ways one experiences oneself. At different times I might see myself as hungry, gratified, weak, or destructively bad. These images (mental self-representations) accumulate over time and, if these images are acceptable, they are organized into a coherent representation of the self as a whole.

However, if these images are intolerable, they must be defended against. For example, if I were intensely hungry, I might fantasize cannibalistically devouring another person: "a young healthy Child, well nursed is, at a year old, a most delicious, nourishing, and wholesome Food; whether *Stewed, Roasted, Baked,* or *Boiled;* and, I make no doubt, that it will equally serve in a *Fricasie,* or *Ragoust.*"[1] But, I may not find this image of myself acceptable. To avoid the guilt of being a murderous cannibal, I might remove myself emotionally from my feasts and observe my self, like on a TV

This paper is a revision of a presentation at the 1979 Modern Language Association Annual Convention's special session on "The Divided Self: Literary and Psychoanalytical Implications of Multiple Personality," December 28, 1979, in San Francisco, California.

© 1984 by The Haworth Press, Inc. All rights reserved.

Dean Martin Roast, as if I were another person eating the roasted child.[2] From another perspective, to avoid an attack because of my non-compliance to others' culinary expectations, I might present what I think the other person expects of me, present my self as a vegetarian, and hide my real eating capacities.[3] Or, since I might fear critical attack because of my cannibalistic successes, I might experience my self as an incompetent, failed cannibal who barely manages to find enough to eat. But, then, to avoid experiencing my self as a mediocre cannibal, I might imagine my self as worthy of a culinary award.[4] Or, fearing that a loved one will not love me and desert me because of my aggressiveness, I might passively, benignly, and benevolently write restaurant reviews to keep the love. Or, if I imagine that I will be smothered and overwhelmed by too much attention because of my benevolent reviews, I might present my self as an aggressive reviewer who pans all restaurants.[5] These ways of defending my "self" as worthy of love, safe from critical and possibly physical attack, and good enough to prevent abandonment, smothering, and guilt, all help me preserve a sense of who I am, even if this sense is distorted, defective, and not adaptive to my potential and interest.

I. One of the most dramatic ways of creating "selves," or personalities, and of particular interest here, appears in multiple personality in which there is present in one person two or more distinct sub-personalities.[6]

Usually, only one personality, the primary, is known by the person; secondary personalities remain hidden from the awareness of the primary personality. Most of us are probably familiar with the case of Sybil, quiet and passive, who was unaware of her fifteen other sub-personalities, one of which was Peggy Lou, an independent, free-willed, aggressive, and angry woman.[7] In the two cases I am personally involved in,* the primary personality is unaware of the secondary, and the two are very much opposites. In the first, Georgia is very masculine in appearance. She wears pants and jackets, acts "cool" and strong, is mostly silent, denies needing anyone for anything, uses drugs, does not like to be touched physically, and swaggers and talks like a 1950s teenage hood. In her poetry she writes, "confidence is my name and coolness my game . . ."

---

*These cases were treated under my supervision by Ms. Donna Gordon, C.S.A.C., Clinic Supervisor, Outpatient Services, Straight and Narrow, Patterson, N.J., in private practice in Washington Township, N.J. She generously contributed much of the case material under consideration here.

Georgina, Georgia's secondary personality, is more feminine. She wears dresses, speaks quietly, likes to be touched sexually, and is warm rather than aloof. Their distinct personalities are not only marked by contrasting dressing habits, by the use of different voices, language, and handwriting, but also by distinct mannerisms. For instance, Georgia is left-handed, Georgina right-handed. In the therapy sessions, when Georgina appears, Georgia shifts her cigarette from her left hand to her right hand.

In the second case, Andrea, the primary personality, is a reserved woman who wants "to make something out of herself" and who talks sweetly. Her secondary personality, Andy, who uses street language, imagines himself as a male, who is into "partying," demanding, careless with money, and does whatever he wants. His voice and mannerisms are more masculine than Andrea's, and he views Andrea as too serious, emotional, and compliant.

II. The most important feature of these sub-personalities, other "selves," is that they are organized personalities. They are not just representatives of psychic structures, like the superego. For instance, Charlie, a sub-personality in Mrs. G., a case reported by Stoller, is described as "her conscience, her superego, her ego ideal, her moral code." Though these characteristics may be present, what is most important is that Charlie is a "character." He "felt like a separate person."[8] Likewise, Sybil's Peggy Lou can be seen as an expression of Sybil's angry, aggressive impulses, as a "projective device . . . permitting a person's forbidden desires to express themselves without having to acknowledge ownership."[8] But, again, it is important to note that a complete person with distinguishing traits and mannerisms, and even with relationships of her own, has been created to embody these feelings. (In fact, these different "personalities" even have differing EEG patterns.)[9,10] With this recognition, it would be difficult to say that the sub-personality represents "chaotic manifestations of the patient's immature part-object representations."[11] Aspects of the sub-personality may concern part-objects, but the mental image of the sub-personality is an image of a whole personality. For example, a patient, later revealed as a multiple personality, has said, "I have split personalities—I don't understand me at all. The real me is a musician who constantly likes to go to church and constantly work. But sometimes the real me is a rough, tough kid who likes riding on motorcycles. I love that image. . . I love my image of being on a motorcycle or a horse. I feel like an outcast."[12] Later, it was revealed that these "images" had names. The "self-images" were multiple selves with different characters.

Since more than one "self" inhabits one body, the primary personality at times is confused. Sybil lost track of time, as does Georgia. They do and say things which they find out about at a later time. Sybil would lose track of days when a sub-personality took over her body; for instance, she "found" her "self" in Philadelphia in a hotel room and could not understand how she had come to be there. This kind of event leads to a basic confusion over "who I am." As Stoller says of Mrs. G., "a crucial identity theme was: 'I do not know who I am . . .'"[8] As Georgia puts it in a poem: "the hardest part of being is being me—I don't know who or what I am anymore." Another poem she signs "Author unknown." Since Georgia generally is dressed in a "man-tailored way," she is confused when she finds herself in dresses and fancy blouses, just as Sybil was confused when she discovered in her closet clothes in a style she disliked.

These other selves develop over time and can be observed at various stages in their development. We can perhaps see a nascent form in one of my patients, Ann, who is not a multiple personality. She reported that in childhood she used to create characters and put them into her head. For instance, she imagined she had a little person inside her head who controlled her brain and dished out guilt by saying, "Who do you think you are!" whenever she was happy. The patient also had created characters out of her hands. Her right hand, named Franny, did "right," that is, whatever her parents wanted her to do. Her left hand, named Zooey,** was mischievous and did what it wanted, not what the parents wanted. The patient experienced these characters as constantly fighting and, since she "needed both," she mediated between the two and tried to make them get along with each other. At times, she was almost incapacitated by her struggle with Franny and Zooey: she could not use her hands and attempted to use her feet to write, eat, and drink. Ann imagines these character or personality traits as "hands," rather than her "self"; but, they are still part of her self. In a multiple personality we can see the intolerable traits imagined as not part of the self. In Georgia, the "left-right" dichotomy develops into a separate "left-self," Georgia herself, and a separate "right-self," Georgina.

**These names have been disguised by the author.

Ann heard these characters' voices, but she was aware that they were part of her. Georgia hears voices which she is unaware of as part of her. This seems to be the next step toward the development of a separate self. In writing of the voices she hears yelling at her, she says, "One makes me shake and tremble with fear./Another is *Right* when I'm left to do wrong." The "right" (Georgina) is associated with "rightness" or "goodness," while the "left" (Georgia) with "wrongness." This parallels my patient Ann and is reminiscent of Eve's faces, one of which is Eve White, where white is right or good.[13] Just as Georgia makes "rightness" into a "voice" and "separate", she similarly experiences her emotions: she speaks of her intense self-hatred, a hate that fights her and hurts her. Her self-hate becomes separate from her "self" and then is imagined attacking that "self" when she says her mind and fists abuse her. Here, the parts of her body are seen to be beginning to be disconnected from her own body and to have a will of their own. We see here a process of development. Ann imagines personality traits as parts of her body, hands; Georgia imagines her body parts having a will of their own and being disconnected from her body proper; then Georgia imagines these "abusers" as "voices," and finally they become other "selves."

Just as there are degrees of "anthropomorphizing" along the road to another "self" (cf. also hallucinations, delusions, imaginary companions), there are varying and fluctuating degrees of awareness of the other "selves." Sybil was at first totally unaware of all her sub-personalities. Georgia seems primarily to view Georgina as another person entirely. She acknowledges that she (Georgia) has a relationship with her lover Sue and that Georgina also has a relationship, of a different quality, with Sue. Georgia knows about Georgina's relationship with Sue because Sue tells her about it. Georgia sees Georgina as a "goody two shoes" who comforts Sue after Georgia has ignored her.

Georgia can, however, become more aware of Georgina's special relationship to her. Asked where Georgina hangs out, Georgia responds "in the mirror." She writes, "She said—'the *Face* in the mirror won't Stop! . . .I'm alive she Cried—Waiting for Me outside!'" The "I" in the poem is Georgia; the "she" is Georgina. Georgia sees Georgina in the mirror, and then confusion over who is who sets in: "I'm alive she Cried—Waiting for Me OUTSIDE!" "I," "she," and "Me" begin to merge, and, curiously, there are no ending quotation marks to the statement by the "she." The narrator, Georgia, and the character, "Georgina" begin to flow together.

In another poem, there is even more recognition that Georgina and Georgia are aspects of the same person: "But I am she and she is Me—"

However, this recognition is not firm or constant. Asked to associate to the poem, Georgia said, "I know what she [Georgina] looks like. She looks like me—just a little bit." In another poem, she has a sense that she has created this other "self" and possibly other "selves": "I wear a thousand masks. . . . Pretending is an art that's second nature with me. . . ." The other patient I am familiar with, Andrea, shows a different kind of awareness, perhaps more of an unawareness. After Andy came to a session to see where Andrea comes for treatment, Andrea came the next time and apologetically and embarrassedly said that "Andy" was only a nickname and that there was only one Andrea. However, Andrea could not remember what Andy had said or where he had sat. This denial of Andy's existence is probably an attempt to keep the therapist (and the patient herself) unaware of this other "self" for defensive purposes.

III. Describing these multiple "selves" is easier than understanding why they come about. It is clear that they protect the person, or "primary personality." But from what? Sybil's "selves," as well as Salama's Kathy's selves[14] were understood as defenses against particular traumatic events of various kinds, while Stoller's Mrs. G. used her other "selves" to express unacceptable impulses and moral codes.[8] However, these explanations do not clarify why this particular dissociative defense is used. Though this question may never be answered, I would like to suggest possibly helpful ways of approaching this problem.

First, one "self," the primary personality, is usually created to meet what the person experiences as the expectations of the important people in her immediate environment. What we have seen in examples of "false selves" and compliant, compulsive personalities, we also saw in Ann's childhood creation of Franny, the "right" hand. We see this kind of self in multiple personalities as well. Andy, the secondary personality, perceives Andrea, the primary, as following society's standards for acceptance and thus as not really being "herself." Georgia, likewise, desires to comply: "I have tried—God knows I've tried/To be more what you expect of me."

Whereas the primary self usually meets others' expectations, the secondary ones are incompatible to both others' and the primary self's expectations. The primary self has, of course, made the expectations of others into her own. Thus, Peggy Lou expressed Sybil's anger, and Charlie expressed Mrs. G.'s moral code. In the cases I am familiar with, Andy displays Andrea's nasty demandingness, and Georgina manifests Georgia's rejected femininity.

Why this split? Why must a person meet another's (and their own) expectations in this way? I suggest it is because she thinks that her life is at stake. It is, literally, a question of "being." Though psychoanalysts generally do not concern themselves with patient's fears of death, a good case has been made that anxiety over death is extraordinarily prevalent in children at an early age and can influence psychopathology.[15,16] Perhaps the best traditional psychoanalytic concept is annihilation anxiety, and not anxiety of loss of love or lowered self-esteem or even "ego disintegration" or "fragmentation." But this annihilation anxiety is not an overwhelming primitive, nonverbal bodily anxiety. Rather it is a conceptualized and fantasized threat capable of being put into words. In speaking of Mrs. G., Stoller focuses on this issue: "She did what she did to survive, to maintain a sense of 'I am'. . . if it meant creating a second personality, she did."[8] Sybil eventually understood this: "When I'm angry, I can't be."[7] Since she cannot exist as her "self," she creates Peggy Lou as a "self" who can be both angry and *be*. As it has been pointed out about Eve White, her "goodness" was the price of her survival.[13] Marmer's "Anne B.," in speaking of her fear of her unconscious, clearly manifests a fear of death—"I will be drowned in it. I'm afraid I'll be electrocuted"—and even fears the analysis will kill her spirit, but Marmer mainly analyzes Anne B.'s fear of the death and loss of her significant objects and her own murderous impulses.[17] In order to get away from childhood traumatic incidents, Georgia has said that she "gave" her childhood experience to Georgina, and in order to save her own life, perhaps threatened because she was a female, Georgia gives up her feminine identity to Georgina. Such a homosexual identity has been tied to a fear of being murdered:

> In the cases of the four children who acted out the fantasy of a homosexual identity, each felt his life was threatened by the parent of the same sex. . . . a paucity of genuine loving feelings led him to conclude that only a change of sex could secure the threatening parent's love and thus save his life.[18]

This desire to be, to survive, is expressed internally in a battle for control, and thus for life, between the primary and secondary selves. Stoller's Mrs. G. acknowledges that the other self wants to take control of her body and mind, while Sybil constantly fears the other "selves." Brende and Rinsley's patient has two "selves" (of five),[19] James and Jay, in a murder-suicide pact: James wants to kill Jay, who wants to die.[3] In both Andrea and Georgia, the multiple selves are in a murderous battle with each other. Andrea first fought a battle with a "voice," and now that the voice has become Andy she battles with him to avoid being taken over. In fact, from Andrea's perspective, Andy does wish Andrea to die. Georgia, likewise, fears that Georgina will take over: "the fight has only just begun/And will continue 'til one has won." Interestingly, at this point in the poem, the handwriting changes, and Georgina *has,* apparently, taken over: "But one of these days I'll get you." The fight to the death appears more overtly in another poem: "I realized this fight would continue till I DIE." Georgia's therapist has observed this deadly struggle over Georgia's body in the therapy session. As Georgina attempts to manifest herself, Georgia's teeth clench, her lips tighten, and her hands grasp the couch. Once, while speaking as Georgia and smoking left-handed, the patient's hands began struggling over the cigarette until the right hand won out and Georgina then appeared.

This internal murderous battle, perhaps, mirrors the patient's earlier childhood experience. Sybil experienced her mother as wanting to murder her. Hoping to be rescued from her murderous environment, she pins her hope on a hospital doctor. But, "when the doctor denied her hope of rescue from without, the rescue came from within. The original child, Sybil, ceased to be."[7] Two other selves were created—Peggy and Vicky. Stoller's Mrs. G. had a similar view of a deadly mother: "My mother's an old woman who wants me to die. . . .She always said, 'I think you'd be better off dead.' "[8] From Andrea's perspective, her father wants to destroy her, abuse her, step on her, and tear her apart. Georgia reports similar experiences. A recent dream indicates her fear and how she handles it. In the dream her friend's mother is going to kill her (Georgia), and Georgia hears voices telling her to kill the mother first; but Georgia does not and, sacrificing herself, is shot. After extensive associations to the dream, Georgia concluded that she did not want to believe that anyone would intentionally want to hurt another person and that, instead of her hurting someone, "it was easier to take the shot.'' Whatever Georgia's actual childhood experience was, what is important is her subjective experience. Real murderous threats need not have occurred. Violence of any kind in her environment, plus her own violent fantasies, may have been enough to intensify her fear of being murdered and her resultant defensive multiple personality (cf. Boor[20], Greaves[21]):

> Whether the fear of infanticide dominated the child's life or became a manageable element depended in large part . . . on the incidence of traumatic events and on the degree of violence and of love he had absorbed from his familial environment. Violence or the threat of violence confirmed his already well-established fears. . . His need for defenses was compounded, however, by his inevitably violent response to his parents' violence . . .[18]

IV. It is interesting to note that Georgia, like Sybil and Marmer's Anne B., uses art to express herself. A silent, withholding person, Georgia says that poetry is the only way she can express what is bothering her and who she is and is not. The themes of the poems express Georgia's everyday psychic concerns—her hurt, pain, confusion, and fears of death. Particularly stressed is the idea of being "whole" or "one" versus falling to "pieces": "Give me *ONE* Euphoric moment . . . Give me *peace*—/ Don't take pieces, of me.'' Here, she seems to have touched her basic problem, but her awareness does not carry over to conscious, rational thought.

Whereas Sybil painted in several styles and Anne B. in different colors, each according to the personality which was operative at the time, Georgia writes in one style and mostly from her own point of view as opposed to Georgina's. But, curiously and appropriately, her handwriting changes according to the personality in force. Usually, most of the poem is written in Georgia's handwriting and occasionally the last few lines are in Georgina's. The content of the last lines reflect the change in personality. There is usually a death threat, like "Pat her on the Head and Wish her Dead.'' In the original, handwritten form the letters at the beginning of the line slant to the right and at the end of the line slant to the left. She has apparently switched hands and personalities in the middle of the line.

Stylistically, Georgia, as might be expected, anthropomorphizes. Birds can be "hurt" emotionally like humans; emotions "scream";

and the night has eyes. Reality itself has human traits which make it capable of "taking walks" and "looking over its shoulder."

Given her "multiple" personality, Georgia, perhaps understandably, makes frequent use of puns, especially those associated with her major concerns regarding her oneness, her fragmentation, and her sense of "I." We have seen her "til one has won," and her play on "peace" and "piece." She also frequently plays on "I" and "eyes." Many of the poems are about what she sees and does not see, about her "glazed eyes." Though she does not see these glazed "I's" in her conscious life, she does seem to see her different "I's" in the poetic puns.

Her artistic expressions, of course, express her impulses and fantasies, but, in addition, both in the content and the form of the poetry, she is involved in defining her "self"—her sense of fragmentation, her sense of oneness, and her sense of identity. In her artistic attempts she seems to illustrate Winnicott's theory of cultural phenomena[22]: she is defining inner and outer, real and unreal, and the boundaries of her self in relation to others.[18] For Georgia, art truly is a definition of the self.

V. In conclusion, the multiple personality makes multiple selves to protect her self from a real or fantasized death threat. From the patient's perspective, the self's existence or being is at stake. Such an extreme dissociation is a response to an extreme threat, while lesser self defense manuevers—such as "false" selves—might be seen as responses to real or fantasized lesser threats. An "organized" personality, the other self has not just one or two traits but is a whole image or representation of a whole person. In fact, in a sense it would need to be. Since the person believes her life as a whole person is threatened by this other person, killing off the other self would save the primary self. In her suicide attempts, Georgia cuts her right wrist, that is, Georgina; killing Georgina would, in fantasy, leave Georgia alive. The multiple personality's awareness of her other selves varies. Georgia seems more aware of her other self as an aspect of herself in her poetry than in her everyday life. However, the way she creates her symptom has parallels with the way she creates her art: she multiplies poetic meanings in one word as she multiplies selves in one body.

REFERENCES

1. Swift, J. A Modest Proposal. (1729) *The Writings of Jonathan Swift.* Ed. R. Greenberg & W. Piper. New York: W.W. Norton, 1973.

2. Frances, A., Sacks, M. & Aronoff, M. Depersonalization: A Self-Object Relations Perspective. *Int. J. Psa.* 58: 325-31, 1977.

3. Winnicott, D. Ego Distortion in Terms of True and False Self. (1963) *The Maturational Processes and the Facilitating Environment.* New York: Int. Univ. Press, 1965.

4. Kohut, H. *The Analysis of the Self.* New York: Int. Univ. Press, 1971.

5. Masterson, J. *The Psychotherapy of the Borderline Adult.* New York: Brunner/Mazel, 1976.

6. Hinsie, L. & Campbell, R. *Psychiatric Dictionary,* 4th edition. New York: Oxford Univ. Press, 1974.

7. Schreiber, F. *Sybil.* New York: Warner, 1973.

8. Stoller, R. *Splitting.* New York: Quadrangle, 1973.

9. Ludwig, A., Brandsma, J., Wilbur, C., Bendfeldt, F. & Jameson, D. The Objective Study of a Multiple Personality. *Arch. Gen. Psych.* 26: 298-310, 1972.

10. Coons, P. et al. EEG Studies of Two Multiple Personalities and a Control. *Archives of General Psychiatry.* 39: 823-25, 1982.

11. Lasky, R. The Psychoanalytic Treatment of a Case of Multiple Personality. *Psa. Rev.* 65: 355-380, 1978.

12. Horton, P. & Miller, D. The Etiology of Multiple Personality. *Comprehensive Psychiatry* 13: 151-59, 1972.

13. Berman, J. The Multiple Faces of Eve and Sybil: *E Pluribus Unum. Psychocultural Rev.* 2: 1-25, 1978.

14. Salama, A. Multiple Personality: A Case Study. *Canadian J. Psychiatry,* 25: 569-72, 1980.

15. Marmer, S. Psychoanalysis of Multiple Personality. *Int. J. Psa.* 61: 439-59, 1980.

16. Yalom, I. *Existential Psychotherapy.* New York: Basic Books, 1980.

17. Searles, H. Schizophrenia and the Inevitability of Death. *Psychiatric Q.,* 35: 631-55, 1961.

18. Bloch, D. *"So the Witch Won't Eat Me": Fantasy and the Child's Fear of Infanticide.* Boston: Houghton Mifflin, 1978.

19. Brende, J. & Rinsley, D. A Case of Multiple Personality with Psychological Automatisms. *J. of the Amer. Acad. Psa.* 9: 129-51, 1981.

20. Boor, M. *A Case History and Comparative Study of a Multiple Personality.* Pittsburgh: Univ. of Pittsburgh, 1981. (ERIC Document Reproduction Service No. Ed 201934)

21. Greaves, G. Multiple Personality: 165 Years after Mary Reynolds. *J. Nervous and Mental Disease.* 168: 577-96, 1980.

22. Winnicott, D. *Playing and Reality.* New York: Basic Books, 1971.

Aggression Victimology: Treatment of the Victim

Irwin L. Kutash

Victims sometimes promote their attack. This must be recognized and new classifications and treatment approaches applied to these and all victims who have been overlooked in the rush to treat offenders. The system presented here is based on studies in four areas—concentration camp survivors, battered children, rape victims, and masochists and on my own clinical work.

Concentration Camp Survivors

Bettelheim (1943), in his account of the concentration camp experience, describes in detail the behavior of the long-term victim, including such key symptoms as apathy, regression, and identification with the aggressor. Krystal (1968) has catalogued many symptoms in the survivor that have been descriptive of traumatic neurosis—such symptoms are irritability, free-floating anxiety, disturbed sleep pattern with recurrent nightmares, retrograde amnesia, neurasthenia, hypochondriasis, and somatization. Neiderland (1968) and Bychowski (1968) add such additional key symptomology to the survivor syndrome description as depression, lowered self-esteem, guilt, inability to handle anger, inability to establish interpersonal relationships, lowered ego strength, and paranoid personality features. Mattucek (1971), in studying late symptomology found that many survivors continue the life-style of a prisoner; they apparently have developed a masochistic life-style. Chodoff (1970) found two symptom groupings in victims: some develop passive and apathetic life-styles; others develop aggressive and paranoid life-styles. Berger (1977) found that some survivors accept the role of the victim while others identify with the aggressor and experience guilt due to conflict over this identification. I have found some of these symptoms transmitted to a child of survivors as part of a family system. Sigal and his associates (1973) also found second-generation effects.

© 1984 by The Haworth Press, Inc. All rights reserved.   *47*

Battered Children

Kempe and his colleagues (1962) coined the term "battered-child syndrome" to describe the children who are physically injured by their parents. This definition of child abuse was expanded by Morris, Gould, and Matthews (1964) and Young (1964) to include neglect, and the definition has now come to include emotional mistreatment. Ounsted, Oppenheimer, and Lindsay (1975) believe that the battered child lacks basic trust; they describe his "frozen watchfulness", manifested in lack of speech or sounds, fixed gaze, and lack of positive affect. Blumberg (1977) describes the battered child as fretful and lethargic, with disturbed sleep and eating patterns and nightmares. Several studies have found that battered children frequently become child abusers as adults (Kempe and others, 1962; Mernick and Hurley, 1969, Oliver, 1971). Significantly, Bender (1976) found that battered children often continue their role as victim with individuals outside the home and may seek abuse all their lives. This dichotomy of identification with the aggressor or development of a masochistic life-style parallels the survivor findings.

Rape Victims

In the area of rape, as in the area of child abuse, studies of the attacker have far exceeded studies of the victim. Factor (1954) has discussed the rape victim's symptom of guilt based on unconscious complicity. Werner (1972) ascribed one rape victim's symptoms of depression (including insomnia, loss of appetite, and crying), fears, anxiety and guilt, to the fact that the rape had turned this victim's fantasy into reality. Burgess and Homstrom (1976) describe traumatic neurosis (in addition to guilt and self-blame) as a possible result of rape. The constellation of symptoms for survivors is again seen. Notman and Nadelson (1976) found that rape heightens the victim's sense of helplessness, intensifies dependency conflicts, generates guilt and self-criticism, and interferes with trusting relationships.

Masochists

The literature on masochism also provides much theoretical and clinical material for the study of aggression victimology, since masochism can obviously be a key factor where complicity or symbiosis between victim and attacker is concerned. Masochism has been studied intensively by psychoanalysts since Freud (1905b, 1924) first described erotogenic masochism (masochistic behavior associated with sexual enjoyment) and moral masochism (behavior associated with a need for punishment from parental figures or from the introjected parental superego). In Reich's (1945) view, moral masochism represents a need for punishment, but it is also a defense to avoid even worse feared punishment if the individual does not submit. Masochism has also been related to the individual's feelings of powerlessness, self-hate and low self-esteem brought on by his having a sadistic mother and fearing her total abandonment if this role is not maintained (Menaker, 1953), and to the individual's characteristic manner of reacting to early conflicts (Berliner, 1958; Brenner, 1959; Eisenbud, 1967). This later group will be emphasized.

In a *Chicago Sun-Times* report on March 6, 1978, Richard Speck admitted killing seven of eight nurses slain twelve years ago and is quoted as stating: "Yeah, I killed them, I stabbed and choked them. If that one girl wouldn't have spit in my face, they'd all be alive today."

He went on to describe the incident in more detail, after explaining he only intended to commit a robbery.

> We didn't pick no house, we just knocked. When people answered the door, we asked for phoney names and left. We were waiting for no one to answer so we could break in and burglarize it. . .We knocked on the girl's door. No one answered. It wasn't planned or nothing. When we got upstairs we seen them all in the bedrooms asleep. . .Some girls woke up. We said, 'Stick up! we want your money!' I told one of them to get the money. She spit in my face and said she'd pick me out of a lineup. Ninety-nine percent of the people in this country are stool pigeons. I just blew. . .I can't even tell you what she looked like, to be truthful. She got stabbed in the heart.

As early as 1948, Hans Von Hentig held that a "nefarious symbiosis" often exists between victims and offenders with the victim stimulating the offender toward a criminal response directed at him. He called these victims "activating sufferers." He felt such victims are of four kinds: (1) those who desire injury (submitting) (2) those who become victims to achieve great gain (conniving) (3) those who cooperate (contributory) and (4) those who provoke or instigate (soliciting). Benjamin Mendelsohn, a Rumanian lawyer and behavior researcher (1963), developed the concept further, dividing victims into six categories based on degree of culpability.

Two early case histories supporting these hypotheses appeared in 1961 and 1963. In 1961, Charles De Leon reported on a woman who killed her friend after he beat her with a chair leg. She had earlier reported to her doctor, "That man outside is going to make me kill him and I really don't want to do anything like that." De Leon concluded that a homicide victim may bring about his own suicide by provoking his killer.

Louis H. Gold, in 1963, describes a patient who concluded:

> Sometimes I think my wife committed suicide using me as an instrument. Why did she leave the pocketbook open with the boyfriend's letter sticking out? She knew she was pregnant, the abortion pills didn't work. It was the second illegitimate pregnancy, it was by another man, she couldn't get rid of it. She knew it wasn't mine because I was sterile. She wanted no more children and I agreed to have the vasectomy in Springfield. She was suicidal during the first illegitimate pregnancy and I talked her out of it. I told her I was going to marry her.

The patient then described this unusual reaction just prior to the shooting:

> When I walked in with that pistol she was very calm and she said, 'You are going to kill me anyway so you may as well do it now.' I really had wanted her to come outside and talk to me but she said that she wasn't going to move. Being killed was her only way out of her terrible situation.

Perhaps the strongest confirmation of the "victimimal behavior" hypothesis can be found in Marvin Wolfgang's study (1970) that 26% of murder victims precipitated their attacks (150 of 588 Philadelphia murder cases). He described a typical case in the following manner:

> A drunken husband, beating his wife in their kitchen, gave her a butcher knife and dared her to use it on him. She claimed that if he should strike her once more, she would use the knife,

whereupon he slapped her in the face and she fatally stabbed him.

Wolfgang found that the victim is often the first party to use physical force. The provocative or precipitating factors could be physical or psychological, overt or covert, or could develop over the years or in a short amount of time. He also concluded that victims could be so apparently provocative that they may even use killers as a means of suicide in some cases.

These behaviors are not limited to adults. In fact, Julius Segal and Herbert Yalraes in a *Psychology Today* article, "Bringing up Mothers," November, 1978, ask, "Do some babies invite abuse?" and conclude that the victims play a role in evoking parental violence.

To truly understand violence, therefore, understanding the offender is not enough. We must also thoroughly understand the other half of the equation, the victim. While some victims are totally innocent of any complicity or provocation, as has been indicated, that is frequently not the case. For this reason, the author has coined the following classifications of victims as part of a new classification and treatment system for victims of violent aggression, which takes into account the victim's role. The entire classification system can be found in Kutash (1978).

Situational Aggression Victims—Victims attacked or murdered due to circumstances beyond their control.

Promotional Aggression Victims—Victims who promoted or invited their own attacks or murders, consciously or unconsciously.

Some of these victims include persons who derive pleasure from pain, who crave punishment to allay guilt or who associate being hurt with being loved or taken care of. Masochists can also be promotional aggression victims.

The disorders that can develop in the situational aggression victim can be of two types, acute or chronic, and each includes a discrete set of symptoms.

Acute Situational Aggression Victim Syndrome—This is a transient situational disturbance which follows a physical attack. Symptoms range from exhaustion, anxiety, grief, disorientation, hostility, remorse, regression and denial, to extreme cases which simulate hysterical neurosis of either a conversion type or a dissociative type. The military used to refer to these latter symptoms as "shell shock" or "battle fatigue."

Chronic Situational Aggression Victim Syndrome—This is a disorder of long duration that develops over a prolonged period of being the victim of aggression. (e.g., prisoners of war or concentration camp inmates). Symptoms range from neurasthenia, chronic anxiety, guilt, irritability, sleep disturbance, retrograde amnesia, extreme apathy, regression, low self-esteem and weak ego strength, to identification with the aggressor, massive hypochondriasis and somatization, and psychotic depressive reactions.

While being a situational aggression victim leads to disorders that weaken ego strength, promotional aggression victims have ego deficits to begin with, which lead to the symptoms of victiming. These disorders can be of three types: impulsive, compulsive or characterological.

Impulsive Promotional Aggression Victim Disorder—This is a transient disorder occurring when an individual receives a severe blow to his ego or self-esteem and immediately endangers himself, either consciously or unconsciously. This may occur after a person loses a job, fails at school or experiences unrequited love. While the disorder may be regretted later, at the moment it occurs it is experienced as pleasurable and irresistible. This reaction may involve adopting the aggressive attitudes towards oneself or the rejecting party, hence seeking punishment, hoping for revenge by taking a "look what you drove me to" stance or a conscious or unconscious attempt to receive if not acceptance, pity.

Compulsive Promotional Aggression Victim Disorder—This is a chronic disorder occurring when a person's early experiences have led him to experience infantile feelings of anxiety or guilt and, as a reaction, he repetitively invites punishment. His victiming is insistent, intrusive and contrary to his wishes but serves as a substitute for still more unacceptable, unconscious wishes. Not victiming, therefore, leads to more anxiety than victiming. This reaction involves a buildup of guilt or anxiety, its diminishing by victiming and then a repetition of this cycle (e.g., he has come to deplore himself for exaggerated sins and victiming leads to temporary relief from the guilt or anxiety.)

Characterological Promotional Aggression Victim Disorder— This is a chronic, habitual, maladaptive disorder occurring when a person has come to associate sexual gratification, gratification of dependency needs or love with physical or psychological pain, and then consciously or unconsciously develops a life style that seeks it out. In other cases, the pleasure may derive from identifying with the aggressor and vicariously satisfying the victim's own aggressive wishes. In this disorder, the pattern of reacting is comfortable to the victim or ego syntonic, as opposed to the compulsive promotional aggression victim whose reactions are uncomfortable or ego alien.

Although these five discrete categories of disorder have been established, and somewhat different treatment approaches will be elucidated for each, these disorders, like all mental disorders are rarely seen in pure form. There is often a somewhat promotional component in the most situational aggression victim, and vice versa. Furthermore, from undergoing prolonged victimage as a chronic situational aggression victim, a person who is not treated can develop a promotional aggression victim disorder.

Society has expended great time and energy in treating offenders but little on treating victims. For this reason new therapies were needed and the author has formulated Situational Aggression Victim Emoto-Restorative Psychotherapy or SAVE Therapy for situational aggression victims and Promotional Aggression Victim Emoto-Remotivational Psychotherapy or PAVE Therapy for promotional aggression victims.

SAVE therapy consists of thorough exploration of the attack and the feelings involved with it and then putting them in the context of the person's overall experiences. Its goal is to restore the victims to their pre-trauma condition. The following is a profile of a typical candidate for this therapy.

A woman I treated had been brutally attacked and raped by a stranger at knifepoint on the way from her job as a buyer for a department store. She had been fortunate in receiving immediate medical attention but had not received any psychological aid. She remembered feeling anxious and disoriented, that no one had talked to her other than to get a statement of what happened, and that no family members were called until she had been at the hospital for several hours. She described herself as too confused and embarrassed to call anyone. Anxiety, a feeling of self-doubt and a fear of going outside persisted for several weeks and she, therefore, came for psychotherapy. Her first words were, "I hope I can talk to you, you're a man. I can't even look at my husband any more."

PAVE therapy includes thorough exploration of the feelings experienced by being a victim and, most importantly, helping him or her become conscious of the unconscious causes of the victiming. After the individual is in touch with the feelings he or she experienced while being victimized, he or she is guided to explore when they experienced these feelings in past relationships and with whom. This can extend back to early childhood with sadistic parents or to early sources of guilt or anxiety. It can lead to the insight that there is no cause to hate oneself or to continue to experience anxiety or guilt for past "sins" that can be alleviated by victiming. It can lead to the discovery that satisfying dependency needs or receiving love is not dependent on victiming or that sexual gratification does not have to be paired with pain but is allowed without a price.

The person is also guided to recognize his part in becoming a victim and the control he or she exercises over it. In reviewing the history of victims, the interpretation can eventually be made that many victimal experiences are more than coincidence. The person in therapy is then free to adopt new behavior that is less self-destructive. The goal of this therapy is to remotivate the individual so as to prevent reoccurrence of victiming, as distinct from SAVE therapy where the therapist is minimizing the adverse emotional effects of victimization. The following is a typical PAVE therapy candidate.

A young man I treated was raised by his mother and aunt after the father deserted the family when the patient was an infant. His mother developed a deep hatred for men and always told him that he was no good, like his father. He accepted this and, in fact, grew up with the dilemma that to be a man was to be no good but not to be a man meant he was abnormal. As early as twelve he remembered contemplating suicide and his failure to do so he described as another example of how weak he was. He remembered as an adult indulging in "half measures," like taking his eyes off the road while driving or walking in Central Park late at night. As an adult he vacillated between relationships where he was eventually rejected by women, or sado-masochistic relationships with men where he took the passive sex role. He felt ashamed, guilty and miserable after each such episode. Once, following an encounter, as he was leaving his partner's apartment building he started berating a group of teenage boys who were blocking the front stairs. Even when they moved aside he described how he kept telling them, "You punks are no good." The boys beat him until he had a broken rib and a concussion and then left him unconscious on the stairs. Shortly after the attack he came for therapy.

Treatment of each of the five aggression victim disorders will now be considered in detail. The focus will be on those methods most specifically applicable to each; however, methods used with victims but also already utilized with other disorders, and already in the literature in that application, will not be discussed in detail.

Treating the Acute Situational Aggression Victim

Three phases are involved in treating the acute situational aggression victim: (1) on-the-scene crisis intervention (when possible); (2) reintegration of the individual into society by utilization of ongoing significant individuals in the victim's life; (3) short-term SAVE Therapy with primary victim and, when necessary, with secondary victims. The goals of this treatment are to limit the effects of the traumatic event and to prevent chronic or permanent emotional disability as an outcome of the attack. In other words, the primary aim is to help the person back to the level of functioning he or she enjoyed prior to the attack. In some cases the goal can exceed this, and actual growth can accrue from the overall trauma and treatment as the victim explores his reaction and successfully overcomes adversity.

On-the-scene treatment of the situational victim of an aggressive attack will, of course, include medical attention, but immediate psychological attention should not be overlooked. In addition to whatever physical harm is done, some immediate psychological symptoms are often apparent, ranging from anxiety, depression and disorientation to hostility, remorse, denial or regression; in extreme cases symptoms of hysterical neuroses, of either a conversion or dissociative type, are apparent.

The very first reaction after the attack is usually anxiety and disorientation. What the victim needs is calm reassurance and reduction of stress while he or she is being removed from the scene. The trauma must not be increased. In severe cases sedation or tranquilization may be necessary but should not be a routine procedure. Many victims can profit from an immediate understanding of exactly what happened and from ventilation of their feelings. If the person is distorting reality, not because of lack of knowledge of what happened but because of the psychological effect of the attack, he should not be contradicted or agreed with. The presence of family or friends at the scene or shortly thereafter should be encouraged or discouraged, depending on whether they increase or decrease the victim's agitation. The family and close friends of an attack victim, if they are not too adversely affected or emotionally disturbed (for instance, the husband who blames his wife for her rape), can be vital in the attack victim's quick recovery. Their warm attitudes can highlight the singular and aberrant nature of the attack. Their acceptance can alleviate the lowering of self-esteem experienced by an attack victim who feels that his or her own flaws led to the attack. If the family members overreact and do not return to the pretrauma status quo or if overprotection is apparent, family counseling may be required.

A rape or physical attack can have psychological effects on people who are emotionally involved with the primary victim; these people, who can be considered the secondary victims of the attack, often need treatment of their own. This possibility certainly should not be overlooked if the primary victim perishes from the attack.

The short-term SAVE Therapy phase is initiated if any symptoms of the situational aggression victim syndrome persist beyond the period of time it takes for physical recovery and when the natural healing process is not taking place. The traumatized victim is helped to ventilate attack-related feelings and to resolve the attack-created conflicts and self-doubts that will not allow him to return to his pre-attack level of functioning. Specifically, the therapist, after getting to know the person and forming a relationship, has the patient describe his or her attack in detail; he then zeros in on the emotions the patient displays in retelling and reflects these feelings to the patient or interprets them. If feelings are not expressed, the therapist asks the patient, "How did you feel while that was occurring or just before the attack or right afterward?" The patient's feelings toward significant others prior to and after the attack are also explored. The person is then guided through an exploration of previous experiences and relationships with people, and, again, the individual's feelings in these relationships are highlighted. In this exploration of the patient's history, the attack is reintegrated into his overall experience; that is, it is put in its proportional place as the exception rather than the rule—an atypical experience.

With children this process can be incorporated into play therapy to help them explore the attack and previous experience. Dolls or puppets can be most effective in playing out events; such role playing may give these children their first real understanding of what happened, their first outlet to discussion of what happened, and their first realization that it is not their fault or a taboo subject.

Treating the Chronic Situational Aggression Victim

Three phases are involved in treating the chronic situational aggression victim: (1) extrication from or treatment of the system in which the victimization occurs; (2) integration or reintegration of the victim into his family or society; (3) long-term SAVE Therapy if the chronic situational aggression victim syndrome is manifested.

Unlike the acute situational aggression victim, the chronic situational aggression victim may still be in the process of being victimized when he or she is first brought to the attention of the therapist. The treatment can involve raising the consciousness of the chronic aggression victim to his victimization, so that he can extricate himself from it or seek appropriate help for his problem. In other situations—for instance, where the victim is a battered child or wife—family therapy or marriage counseling may be required in order to treat the system in which the victimization is occurring. Those cases where a person is being victimized, rather than promoting victimage, but needs help to get out of chronic victimage are hard to separate from cases where the victim is partially culpable or masochistic. In fact, the chronic situation victim may develop into a promotional victim.

Treatment for prisoners of war or concentration camp victims, whom the therapist sees only after their extrication, focuses on helping the individual become psychologically ready to regain his former place in society. Where the victim has been separated from family or wife, family therapy or marriage counseling may be essential along with the victim's own individual treatment. If the victim is unmarried and remains untreated, his future family and children may need these modalities along with the victim, because the victimal personality of the survivor may affect those he is closely involved with.

Long-term victimage, except for those with the strongest premorbid ego, can lead to a discernible lowering of ego strength and self-esteem and personality characteristics that accompany it. In many cases the result is the chronic situational aggression victim syndrome, necessitating a long-term SAVE Therapy. In long-term SAVE Therapy, developing a therapeutic alliance can be difficult, and forming a trusting relationship as a prelude to successful therapy can take a long time, since the therapist must prove his reliability, interest and trustability and must work through initial transferences to authority figures. The therapy itself involves thorough exploration of the victimage and the feelings involved with it and then putting it in the context of the person's overall experience, requiring extensive exploration of his past.

Most long-term SAVE Therapy patients have had a normal developmental history before being set back by prolonged victimage. The therapy in these cases is, therefore, a rebuilding therapy. Another group of chronic aggression victims, however, are the long-term victims of child abuse or concentration camp survivors whose victimage began before their egos were fully developed. In these cases a building form of therapy, as opposed to a rebuilding is necessitated. In addition to therapy, a therapeutic milieu in which the child can build his ego is essential.

If treated during childhood, a battered child may be discovered while still in the situation of chronic victim. Untreated, he or she may develop into a promotional aggression victim as an adult, expending great effort to find relationships like his early relationships. A battered wife, for instance, may have been abused as a child. She may have had a "warm" father who beat and abused his children when he was intoxicated; she therefore sought and found a husband who would provide what she was accustomed to, or had learned to feel she deserved, or had come to associate with more positive aspects of her relationships with her parents.

Battered children can be spotted by professionals in schools, clinics or doctors' offices with repeated physical signs of abuse or emotional signs of psychological abuse. In some such cases the pathological family is open to being treated as an entity; in others the victim must be removed from the traumatic environment, usually through legal action by social agencies. Replacement with a therapeutic milieu and therapy to "work through" these early damaging experiences must follow.

SAVE Therapy with adults must involve exploration of their experience, in order to rebuild their ego strength and to reintegrate them into society. SAVE Therapy with children involves exploration of their traumatic experience, along with more healthy experiences, as part of a relationship therapy, designed to build ego strength. It allows the child to go through developmental stages with the therapist at the same time as a therapeutic milieu is provided, where social ties and identifications can occur.

Treating the Impulsive Promotional Aggression Victim

The treatment approach for the impulsive promotional aggression victim includes (1) on-the-scene crisis intervention (when possible); (2) reintegration of the individual into preexisting relationships of a positive nature; (3) short-term PAVE Therapy with the victim and short-term SAVE Therapy with secondary victims when necessary.

The impulsive promotional aggression victim, unlike the acute situational aggression victim, has placed himself in a situation where he could become a victim in reaction to being rejected by significant others. Therefore, this type of victim must be helped to understand his motivation (to punish someone who has spurned him, by creating guilt or regret in this rejecting person, or to punish himself for being so "unworthy") and to recognize different possible reactions to future rejections. The goals of this treatment are to prevent the repetition of the invitation to be aggressed against and to help remotivate the victiming individual desirous of change.

In addition to the steps already described for on-the-scene treatment of the acute situational aggression victim, the impulsive promotional aggression victim must be observed and, if necessary restrained, since he may escalate his victiming. His anger may grow if his victiming does not have the desired effect on the person who delivered the blow to his ego or self-esteem and thereby precipitated his impulsive victiming.

The impulsive promotional aggression victim has several identifiable features. Rather than being anxious or disoriented as a first reaction to being attacked, he may show signs of relief of tension. He may, if depressed or hostile, display regret or hostility—not toward the attacker or even, as the situational aggression victim might, toward the helper, but toward a party who is not even on the scene. Finally, he may provoke further attack. In these cases utilization of family and close friends can be important to show the person that he or she is cared for, if that is the case. If destructive ongoing relationships exist, family therapy or marriage counseling is indicated.

If the victim can be motivated to enter therapy, a short-term PAVE Therapy phase should be initiated immediately following the first identifiable victiming. In this phase the victim is helped to ventilate the feelings that led him to invite the attack as well as his feelings during the attack, and to explore the often unconscious cause of the victiming, the victim's fantasied results, and the actual results. The victim is then helped to discover alternatives leading to new motivations. Analysis of the results from their victiming, as opposed to their fantasied results, often motivates these victims to seek a different solution to similar circumstances in the future. If the victim got the desired effect, such as shows of affection or regret, he must be helped to realize that positive feelings in others were there with or without the victiming.

When the individual has repeatedly put himself in danger in an impulsive fashion following rejection, he must be guided to identify antecedent events and feelings: "If I am rejected, I feel tense and irritable; then I put myself in danger." Once the person sees that A (I am rejected) leads to B (I feel tense) and then C (I impulsively begin victiming), he can catch himself at A or B. This approach of building in a barometer for future dangerism is a technique also of great utility with compulsive promotional aggression victims.

Treating the Compulsive Promotional Aggression Victim

The treatment for compulsive promotional aggression victims is long-term PAVE Therapy, because their disorder—like that of the characterological promotional aggression victim—developed over a lifetime and is firmly ingrained. With compulsive promotional aggression victims, however, the prognosis is far better than with the characterological promotional aggression victims, because the symptoms are ego alien rather than ego syntonic. The guilt and anxiety that motivate these victims to victiming can also motivate them to therapy, because they get only temporary relief through victiming.

The therapy with both compulsive promotional aggression victims and characterological promotional aggression victims includes exploring the victim's feeling during victimage and making conscious the unconscious meaning of these victiming actions and feelings. Such standard psychoanalytic techniques as relating the past to the present, dream analysis, analysis of transference, and free association are utilized to bring into the person's awareness and understanding the latent as well as the manifest motivations of his actions. The person is then guided to an understanding of his own irrational or no longer rational motivations, leading to remotivation and normal functioning.

In PAVE Therapy with compulsive promotional aggression victims, the victim may consciously experience guilt but be unconscious of its origin due to repression. He will, to gain temporary relief from guilt, put himself down as well as invite punishment from others. These persons show low self-esteem and what has been referred to as an "inferiority complex." They may even justify and rationalize the acts of aggression against them. The therapist must lead these victims back to their infantile fantasies, especially to aggressive fantasies that have been repressed due to fear of exaggerated consequences. These feelings must be made conscious—through free association, dream analysis, and examination of feelings during past victiming behavior—and then ventilated. The person must discover that he has done nothing wrong, or else he will compulsively promote his own punishment, be accident prone, have foreboding feelings, be unable to handle success, be oversolicitous of others, or become a martyr in order to atone. He may even become a criminal in order to be caught and punished.

As has been seen, the compulsive promotional aggression victim may compulsively and repetitively invite attack to atone for unconscious guilt feelings. Exploration of the victim's history can bring about the insight that the victimage is more than coincidence and that he has had a part in promoting it. By zeroing in on the feelings during the victiming and asking the person when he experienced these feelings before, the therapist can help the victim get back to these previous incidents—perhaps all the way back to childhood experiences with parents. Associating to the feelings in dreams may have the same effect. Once the pattern is identified and the victim is conscious of it, he has the option of acting differently, since the compulsion is diminished. The technique of identifying antecedent events and feelings to the victiming, to building in a barometer of when victiming may again occur, can be effective in this regard.

Treating the Characterological Promotional Aggression Victim

In the characterological promotional aggression victim disorder, the prognosis is worse than in all previous disorders discussed. The characterological promotional aggression victim associates satisfaction of dependency needs, love or sexual gratification with pain. Since these victims are less likely to feel anxiety and depression than those in the other categories, they are less motivated to change or seek treatment. The nature of the victiming does not often lead to contact with professionals who will steer them to therapy. Since victiming is their life-style, an "on-the-scene" phase of treatment is ruled out. Utilization of family or close friends can be counterproductive unless they are motivated toward changed relationships, and they are often an integral part of the pattern. Sometimes, however, PAVE Therapy can get the person in touch with the feelings he experiences in his victiming life-style and then explore where else or how else he can experience such satisfaction of needs, love or pleasure. For several possible reasons, these victims have never experienced many normal outlets for gratification: (1) Their self-concept will not allow them to seek different types of acquaintances (2) They have great quantities of anger, which—in their masochism—get turned inward (3) Their early experiences tied satisfaction of dependency needs, love or sexual pleasure with pain and led them to the unconscious deal, "I must experience pain to be allowed satisfaction of dependency needs, love or sexual pleasure."

Some characterological promotional aggression victims may invite aggression or live in a masochistic life-style because, throughout their early development, they were shown attention and concern primarily after they were injured or abused or while they were ill. Here again, the unconscious origin of their masochism must be unearthed through insight-oriented analytic techniques, and new motivations discovered or alternative "healthier" ways found to fulfill their needs.

Other characterological promotional aggression victims, while also seeking punishment or displeasure, achieve sexual pleasure from being punished or humiliated. This makes the condition less responsive to treatment. These victims often identify with the sadistic aggressor and thereby satisfy their own sadistic impulses or infantile needs for power or control. Where pain and humiliation are perceived as pleasurable in and of themselves by the victim, the prognosis is especially poor. It is somewhat better in cases where pain is a prerequisite for sexual gratification or where the patient has a masochistic character trait and enjoys his power over the aggressor but does not enjoy the pain itself. In these cases the victim can learn that pain is not a price one must pay to enjoy sexual pleasure. Once this equation is conscious, his aggression can find direct constructive outlets as he develops greater ego strength. In contrast, those who find pain pleasurable are being treated to give up something they enjoy and will see no gain in doing so, except if driven to treatment by the law or medical factors. The person must discover that what he desires can be had in less self-defeating or even in self-enhancing ways.

BIBLIOGRAPHY

Bender, B. "Self-Chosen Victims: Scapegoating Behavior Sequential to Battering." *Child Welfare*, 1976, 17, 417-422.

Berger, M. "The Survivor Syndrome: A Problem of Nosology and Treatment", *American Journal of Psychotherapy*, 1977, 31, 238-251.

Berliner, B. "Role of Object Relations in Moral Masochism", *Psychoanalytic Quarterly*, 1958, 27, 38-56.

Bettelheim, B. "Individual and Mass Behavior in Extreme Situations." *Journal of Abnormal and Social Psychology,* 1943, 38, 417-452.

Blumberg, M. "Treatment of the Abused Child and the Child Abuser", *American Journal of Psychotherapy,* 1977, 31, 204-215.

Brenner, C. "The Masochistic Character." *Journal of the American Psychoanalytic Association,* 1959, 7, 197-226.

Bullard, D. "Failure to Thrive in the Neglected Child", *American Journal of Orthopsychiatry,* 1967, 37, 680-689.

Burgess, A. and Holmstrom, L. "Coping Behavior of the Rape Victim", *American Journal of Psychiatry,* 1976, 133:4, 413-417.

Bychowski, G. "Permanent Character Changes as an After-Effect of Persecution." In *Massive Psychic Trauma,* H. Krystal (Ed.) New York, International Universities Press, New York, 1968.

Chodoff, P. "The German Concentration Camp as a Psychological Stress". *Archives of General Psychiatry,* 1970, 22, 78-87.

Eisenbid, R. J. "Masochism Revisited". *Psychoanalytic Review,* 1967, 54, 561-582.

Factor, M. "A Woman's Psychological Reaction to Attempted Rape", *Psychoanalytic Quarterly,* 1954, 23, 243-244.

Freud, S. "Three Contributions to the Theory of Sexuality" In J. Strachey (Ed.) *The Complete Psychological Works of Sigmund Freud,* Vol. 7, London, Hogarth Press, 1905, 157-160.

Freud, S. "The Economic Problem in Masochism" In J. Strachey (Ed.) *The Complete Psychological Works of Sigmund Freud.* Vol. 19, London: Hogarth Press. 1924, 157-170.

Herjanic, M. and Meyer, D., "Psychiatric Illness in Homicide Victims", *American Journal of Psychiatry,* 1976, 133:6, 691-693.

Hunt, M. *The Mugging,* New York, New American Library, Inc. 1972.

Jenkins, R., et al. "Interrupting the Family Cycle of Violence", *Journal of the Iowa Medical Society,* 1970, 60:2, 85-89.

Kempe, C. H. or Werman, B. F., Steek, B. F., Droegemueller, Ward Scher, H. K. "The Battered Child Syndrome", *Journal of the American Medical Association,* 1962, 181:7, 17-24.

Krystal, H. "The Problem of the Survivor" In *Massive Psychic Trauma,* H. Krystal, Ed. New York, International Universities Press, 1968.

Krystal, H. and Niederland, W. G. "Clinical Observations on the Survivor Syndrome." In *Massive Psychic Trauma.* H. Krystal, Ed. New York, International Universities Press, 1968.

Kutash, I. L. "Treating the Victim of Aggression." In I. K. Kutash, S. B. Kutash, and L. B. Schlesinger (Eds.), *Violence: Perspectives on Murder and Aggression.* San Francisco: Jossey-Bass, 1978.

Kutash, I. L., Kutash, S. B., and Schlesinger, L. B. *Violence: Perspectives on Murder and Aggression.* San Francisco: Jossey-Bass, 1978.

Mattucek, P. "Late Symptomatology Among Former Concentration Camp Inmates." In *The World Biennial of Psychiatry and Psychotherapy,* S. Arieti, Ed. New York, Basic Books, 1971.

Mendelsohn, B. "The Victimology", *Etudes Internationales de PsychoSociologie Criminelle* 1956, Cited in M. Hunt, The Mugging, New York, New American Library Inc. 1972.

Mendelsohn, B. "The Origin of the Doctrine of Victimology". *Excerpta Criminologica,* 1963, 3:3. 239-244.

Menaker, E. "Masochism—A Defense Reaction of the Ego", *Psychoanalytic Quarterly,* 1953, 22, 205-220.

Mernick, B. and Hurley, J. "Distinctive Personality Attributes of Child Abusing Mothers." *Journal of Counseling and Clinical Psychology,* 1969, 33:6, 746-749.

Morriss, M., Gould, R. and Matthews, P. "Toward Prevention of Child Abuse." *Children,* 1964, 11, 55-60.

Notman, M. and Nadelson, C. "The Rape Victim: Psychodynamic Considerations." *American Journal of Psychiatry,* 1976, 133:4, 408-412.

Oliver, J. and others. "Five Generations of Ill-Treated Children in One Family Pedigree." *British Journal of Psychiatry,* 1971, 119, 473-480.

Ounsted, C., Oppenheimer, R. and Lindsay, J. "Aspects of Bonding Failure: The Psychopathology and Psychotherapeutic Treatment of Families of Battered Children." *Developmental Medicine and Child Neurology,* 1974, 16, 447-456.

Reich, W. "The Masochistic Character." In *Character Analysis.* W. Reich, New York, Orgone Institute Press. 1945.

Sigal, J. J., Silver, D., Rakoff, V. and Ellin, B. "Some Second-Generation Effects of Survival of the Nazi Persecution." *American Journal of Orthopsychiatry,* 1973, 43, 320-327.

Steele, B. F. and Pollock, C. B. "A Psychiatric Study of Parents Who Abuse Infants and Small Children." In R. E. Helfer and C. H. Kempe. Eds. *The Battered Child.* Chicago, University of Chicago Press. 1968. 103-147.

von Hentig, H. *The Criminal and His Victim.* New Haven, Yale University Press. 1948.

Werner, A. "Rape: Interruption of the Therapeutic Process", *Psychotherapy: Theory, Research and Practice,* 1971, 9, 349-351.

Wolfgang, M. *The Sociology of Crime and Delinquency,* New York, John Wiley and Sons, 1970.

Young, L. *Wednesday's Children: A Study of Child Neglect and Abuse.* New York, McGraw Hill, 1964.

Robert Lindner and the Case of Charles: A Teen-Age Sex Murderer: "Songs My Mother Taught Me"

Robert C. Lane

There has been renewed interest in the writings of Robert Lindner with the republishing of his book, *The Fifty-Minute Hour,* [11] by Jason Aronson, Inc., including an introduction by Dr. Robert Langs. The book contains a chapter titled "Songs My Mother Taught Me" about a young murderer named Charles. Lindner, who was particularly known for his penetrating work with psychopaths and psychotics, as well as his psychoanalytic contributions, was a staunch advocate of the importance of Rorschach content. [4-9,12] Each of his papers reiterated that content analysis was one of the "seriously neglected" aspects of Rorschach testing "even though such analysis appears to yield its most important and fertile insights into personality." [6] Lindner felt that content could only be understood through the patient's free association. He wrote:

> The Rorschach examination is a process of continuous disclosure. Onto the raw undifferentiated, plastic and manipulable matter which the blots present, the examinee projects the end products of his internal performing. This material emerges in a form suitable for analysis, but only after it has passed through the refining exercises demanded of all psychological products. What the original impression of the blot stimulus is in any given case can only be discovered through patient retrogressive exploration by free association. [8]

Before discussing the Rorschach of Charles, the patient mentioned

© 1984 by The Haworth Press, Inc. All rights reserved.

in the title of this paper, a summary of the case is in order to acquaint the reader with him.

Charles' parents' marriage was in serious trouble before Charles was born. Religious compulsion permitted the continuation of the marriage until Charles was approximately three years of age. At that time some religious dispensation permitted parental separation and eventual divorce. The father disappeared and the mother told Charles and his younger brother that their father had died. Charles did not discover his father was alive, remarried, and living with his new family in another city until he was thirteen and read some of his mother's secreted personal letters. After Charles' father left the family, his mother made a brief and weak attempt to accept her family burden. She then placed both of her children into an orphanage, supposedly on the advice of a religious counselor. There is a single reference to the brother made by Lindner that the mother "alternated" her visits with her two sons and that they were never with her at the same time. In short, there was no brother-brother relationship. Charles spent his entire life from the age of three until he entered jail in orphanages, foster homes and institutions. In his first foster home placement at the age of four, Charles was beaten "unmercifully" for the smallest infraction and this behavior became pretty much the pattern for his placements.

Specific placements were emphasized by Lindner mainly to point out Charles' uncontrollable behavior. In a number of these instances, the behavior was precipitated by some sexual event in relation to his mother. The first of these described by Lindner occurred when Charles was not quite nine and his mother took him home for Christmas. Before this time, he saw his mother infrequently except for birthdays or holidays. He was overwhelmed by her closeness, fragrant smell and softness when she came to pick him up and kissed him on the lips. Charles dates the first time he felt "sick" back to this event. In his mother's bedroom there were all kinds of feminine secrets, "mysterious vials and bottles," the trunk under the window covered with a shawl and colored cushions with all his mother's treasures inside, and the bed with its satin spread in the middle of the room. Charles looked at and examined everything expecting to be discovered at any moment. He was still at the apartment New Year's Eve when his mother was to give a party. She told him he would have to sleep in her bed. During the night, he was lifted from the bed by a man and brought to the living room couch. He heard voices and laughter in his mother's locked bedroom. It would appear that this primal scene betrayal was related to his acting like a "demon" possessed when he returned to the foster home feeling he had nothing, certainly not his mother's love.

He ran away from foster homes frequently and would end up at his mother's apartment begging for acceptance and becoming more and more curious about her possessions, which he used as transitional objects. At age eleven, he ran away from one foster home and was repeatedly raped by three hobos. Following this incident Charles was once again incorrigible. He spent his twelfth and thirteenth years in another foster home. Lindner reports that Charles, in a visit to his mother's home shortly after his thirteenth birthday, explored his mother's trunk, uncovered all of its contents, including her wedding ring which he found in one of the boxes in the trunk. He was to use the ring to carry out his masturbation ritual. He probed the secrets of the trunk each day and on several occasions would take a ten dollar bill. It was at this time that he learned the truth about his father. He carried the ring in his pocket the last day of his visit until it was time for him to meet his mother, who was to return him to the Protectorate. He put back the ring and took another ten dollar bill. Between Charles' thirteenth birthday and the summer of that year his mother was again called to the orphanage to change his placement. He returned home to the trunk that was waiting for him. Once again he went to the metal box looking for the wedding ring and using it to awaken his sexuality.

From the age of thirteen to fifteen (nearly two years), Charles was sent to a sixty-acre farm run by a rigid middle-aged couple, about whom Lindner said, their only claim to parenthood was that "they once raised a prize bull." Charles was silent most of the time and appears to have been quite depersonalized. Lindner couldn't understand Charles' passivity and acquiescence to this placement in contrast to his violent behavior in other placements. He seemed more content on the farm with the animals and doing his chores. What kept Charles going for two years was his fantasy about and preoccupation with the trunk and the ring. One day he just walked away from the farm and returned to his mother's apartment. He was to repeat the much-fantasized experience which now "had become nuclear in his life." Lindner wrote, "each day, at least once and often many times, he repeated the ceremony until it was fixed as a ritual."

Charles stole money from his mother's pocketbook until he accumulated enough to visit "The Block," an area in town consisting of bars, gin mills and loose sexuality. He was approached at a bar by a prostitute with whom he was impotent until he suggested she wear his mother's ring which he carried in his pocket.

Charles couldn't stay with his mother; there was no room, she would worry, she wasn't available, she couldn't permit it. There is no indication anywhere in Lindner's story that any warm or positive emotional relationship ever existed between mother and son. She was a fairy princess and he, her adoring audience. Charles obtained a position with the Red Cross which lasted only three weeks.

His mother then placed him in an industrial school where he remained from approximately sixteen to past his seventeenth birthday. He was described as a tormentor, wolf, bully, sadist, a swaggering tough who devised a plan which he executed to perfection to get into the "hatchery" where the more privileged citizens, such as the tougher boys, the monitors and assistants, had their own private rooms. This special group privately shared cigarettes, horseplay, smutty stories, perverted sexuality and the plots hatched for power struggles. Charles entered the forbidden area, seized one of the boys whom he stripped with his pen knife, and then carved his initials on the boy's skin. Lindner couldn't understand why Charles ran away from this placement despite being the undisputed dictator and having every possible privilege. The pull to his mother and the masturbation ritual were just too strong. He refused to leave his mother and worked as a Western Union Messenger for several weeks. He was fired because he couldn't be located most of the time. Several days after losing this position, he arose in the morning half-dazed and turned to the trunk, which he now couldn't open. He borrowed a hammer and ice pick from the janitor which he placed on top of the refrigerator when the bell rang. He let in a young girl carrying samples of religious books and records. He told her his mother was in the bedroom. He followed her in, taking the tools. He struck her on the head with the hammer, stabbed her sixty-nine times with the ice pick and then flung himself on her corpse and raped her. Without cleaning the blood off his clothing and body he left the house, "crossed the long bridge across the river," bought an ice cream cone, hitched a ride back across the bridge, and turned himself in to the police.

We have Lindner's report on the case of Charles[10] and Charles' Rorschach administered some years later published in "The Psychoanalytic Review"[13] and I would like to attempt the task of analyzing the content by relating each response to the analytic material concerning Charles described by Lindner. This paper is presented as a tribute to Lindner's astute psychological acumen. (I wish to express my appreciation to Dr. Edward S. Penzer and Dr. Irving Solomon for their helpful comments.)

Charles' reaction of deep shock to the first Rorschach card (300 seconds) revealed an extremely cautious, distrustful and suspicious individual. Such reactions are most typical of the severely depressed and/or the schizophrenic, and Charles had features of both diagnoses. His masochistic defense was highlighted by his self-critical comments, apologetic nature, and general difficulty in responding. Such masochism and general caution Schafer[16] felt often mask expressions of hostility towards the tester and more sadistic and paranoid material. One would be suspicious of this degree of caution and concerned with what it might possibly mask.

Lindner makes the following statement:

> Charles found himself regarding his person and his being with guilt; for under the warped codes and philosophies to which he was exposed he was forced to accept the idea that what was happening to him—his exile from normal life, his abandonment by his family—was somehow his own fault.

Following Charles' initial Rorschach comments to Card I he offers three responses all of a very vague nature: 1) the mouth of a river 2) shadows from trees and 3) part of a map, peninsulas (in the inquiry about the responses given after the showing of all cards).

Charles loses no time in getting to the heart of his problem, the primary fixation points in his object relations and psychosexual development. His immediate turning to the two humps (mouth of a river), so often seen as breasts, suggests a strong oral fixation. Lindner had much to say about this, for Charles stabbed his victim sixty-nine times in the breast and when Charles was under sodium pentathol and asked by Lindner why the breasts, he responded, "make milk." Lindner did not ask, "Why sixty-nine times?," but we know soixante-neuf is a mutual sucking experience. Lindner felt that Charles' violent attack on him was triggered by Charles touching his shoulder, which "felt like a woman's breast." Charles' early masturbation excitement associated with a sick, nauseous, dizzy feeling, involved lying on his mother's bed, pushing aside the silk spread, and pressing his face into the "cleft between the pillows." Charles' comments about his mother's squeezes and hugs when she came to visit him and his comments about women in general concerned their "big bosoms." Lindner's description of the prostitute scene emphasized how excited Charles became when she guided his hands over her breasts. His response, "the mouth of a river," symbolically the vagina, could also be the cleavage between his mother's breasts, and reflects a mouth, breast, vagina (and anus) equation. It is interesting to note that after Charles killed his victim, he "crossed the long bridge over the river." Charles offers two river responses on the Rorschach, suggesting the possibility of a urethral problem, although Lindner did not mention this area in his story.

Charles lacked object constancy and essentially wanted to reunite himself with the mother. He liked to play the game "Going Home" with Lindner (Q—"When are you gonna take me with you?" A— "When hair grows on the Warden's head.").

Shadows on the Rorschach suggest free floating anxiety, depersonalization and often appear in the records of hallucinating patients. Lindner pointed out Charles' auditory hallucinations ("kill, kill") when Charles was under sodium pentathol and again when Charles attacked him. Lindner's words concerning children with long histories of being institutionalized and who move from one foster home to another are most expressive of the succession of transitory episodic life experiences.

> They grow as weeds in a desert, stretching this way and that for sustenance, twisting themselves out of their natural design, mocking Nature's blueprint. They are exposed, more than others, to the vagaries of the human elements, now stifled in the heat of emotional suns, now frozen under loveless snows, now drowned, now parched.

Elsewhere, Lindner speaks of Charles saying, "I never felt a goddamned thing was mine, nothing belonged to me. It always felt like I was borrowing it. . .and if you feel nothing belongs to you then maybe you don't know who you are. . .I mean it's always someone else, like wearing a costume in a play. . .Especially if it's like it was with me. . .You see, I never had nothing that could tell me who I was. . .Even my bed wasn't mine." Additionally, he stated, "I didn't feel like I was alive most of the time," and "I was like a block of wood," and "I got to thinking of myself like one of the horses or pigs around the place." The Red Cross Office Manager under whom Charles had worked commented about Charles, "He seemed to be in a trance most of the time. . .very vague."

Shadows are undifferentiated, amorphous and suggest a very primitive stage of ego development. Lindner realized he did not have an autonomous patient with an independent ego. Charles had to be helped to reach the stage of individuation. The wish for merger with the symbiotic libidinal object was too strong and, as such, there was a retreat to the oral position, with the usual search for passive oral pleasure that accompanies lack of healthy object constancy. Lindner referred to Charles as "ego-less."

> So he became, for all intents, ego-less, an individual without a separate identity, hence a creature—not a person. His role, that is to say, was never a stable one, it shifted from moment to moment as instinctual pressures (and social demands), lacking the mediation normally provided by a balancing "I," fought for dominance in action.

Charles, in talking about his lack of a sense of self, said, "I couldn't find out about myself from inside because she got rid of me too fast, so I had to have things to—to tell me—who I was, and, I didn't even have that." Lindner's classic words in describing the genesis of alienation are as appropriate today as when he first stated them.

> Rejected either actually (as he had been) or by parental attitudes of neglect, self-preoccupation, fear or anxiety, or, on the other hand, apprehensively clutched too closely by emotionally starved parents, the infantile ego never achieves independent identity or that emergent sense-of-self necessary for individual and social maturity. It then is forced to seek selfhood from without, from "things" that serve as referents.

Shadows also depict, like flickering flashes or images, the trauma Charles experienced in his life; Charles' entire life was one trauma after another. It was no wonder he had "mechanically sealed off" the traumatic incidents.

His "peninsula" response indicates both his sense of isolation and wish for grandiosity since a peninsula juts out ahead of the rest of the mainland. Lindner speaks of Charles' first fantasies being heroic and chivalrous, and then giving way to fantasies of revenge

("Richard Coeur de Lion was replaced by Genghis Khan"). A good example of Charles' grandiosity was his taking over the position of "undisputed" leader at the Industrial Home. Lindner describes Charles' behavior at this institution as, "A virtually unopposed dictator. . .he lived the life of a young potentate." The jutting out of the peninsula also suggests a feeling of being different and having repeatedly to test his environment.

The phallic quality of the "peninsula" response (sounds like penis) also lets us know that when Charles retreated and daydreamed, he turned to his penis and fantasies about it for comfort. This was one activity over which he had complete mastery, which he could do by himself, to himself and for himself. Charles had a narcissistic nucleus, a narcissistic investment in and love for the penis, which was an integral part of his psyche.

Charles saw, "Two animals either fighting or kissing. . .doing one of the two," to Card II. This response reflects the projection of his extreme ambivalence to his mother. She is at the same time someone to kiss and love and someone to fight with and hate. Charles' wish for the breast and the deeper wish to merge with his mother on one hand, and his wish to destroy that which he loved on the other, is very clearly described by Lindner. Lindner said, "At the same time that he looked forward to her visits and dreamed of her after she had gone, part of him hated her too, for having placed him in the purgatory of his daily life." To Bleuler[1], this emotional ambivalence, to be able to love and hate at the same time, was an indication of schizophrenia. Lindner related Charles' casting about "for victims on whom to vent himself" to the visits of his mother ("every visit was followed by a display of aggression. . .") and her repeated rejection of him ("his mother's consistent refusal to permit the boy to live with her").

Lindner spent much time discussing "the two-sided nature" of Charles' feelings about his mother. He asked Charles, "Isn't it kind of strange that you kept going back there? Especially when she's never let you stay very long and always turned you back in." To Lindner, Charles represented "a drama of incest and matricide." The murder (killing and raping the girl) was symbolically both "destroying and possessing his mother." Lindner wrote:

> So far as the crime itself was concerned, it was obvious that the intended (psychologically, the real) victim of murder was

not the unhappy girl Charles killed. She was but the substitute, the unfortunate innocent bystander in a drama of incest and matricide whose origins were removed almost two decades from the time the last scene was played.

Perhaps, the clearest manifestation of Charles' sexual conflict and ambivalence regarding his mother occurred when he was nine years of age. These events are summarized:

One of the Sisters calling him to inform him his mother was visiting him; she had come to take him home for the Christmas holidays. Lindner says, "He stood before her his face flushed and his cheeks feeling as if branded with the imprint of her gloved hands where she held them while she kissed his lips, his senses overwhelmed by her sweet perfume and the thick softness of the fur coat she wore."

His taking a bath and lying in his mother's bed, watching her dress for the New Year's Eve party at their home. The tremendous excitement of anticipating her return to the bed during the night was too much for him and forced him to leave the bed and to sleep on the trunk. During the night, he had returned to the bed in a stupor, and had a vague memory of a man lifting him out of the bed and placing him on the sofa, the man then entering his mother's bedroom and locking the door behind him.

Charles tattooing "True Love" on his fingers with a pin following the return to the Home. It is interesting that at this time he is described as having become a "demon." Lindner states, "by the age of 10, he had become perverted in every way to the roots of his being."

Lindner spoke of Charles as "the target of assaults sexual and physical." He particularly described in detail Charles' homosexual abuse at age eleven by three hobos, which led to Charles' hospitalization, and his becoming the butt of sadism which makes a small boy's life a hell. Lindner said he "suffered brutality beyond description, living in constant fear and terror." Freud[2] wrote of the child going from "the passivity of the experience to the activity of the game," and inflicting on others the unpleasure he experienced.

If the doctor looks down a child's throat or carries out some small operation on him, we may be quite sure that these frightening experiences will be the subject of the next game; but we must not in that connection overlook the fact that there is a yield of pleasure from another source. As the child passes over from the passivity of the experience to the activity of the game, he hands on the disagreeable experience to one of his playmates and in this way revenges himself on a substitute.

Charles' repetition compulsion and wish for mastery are eloquently conveyed by Lindner in the following passage:

Toward those smaller and weaker he behaved as he could not toward those larger and stronger. He passed on his hurts; he became an afflictor, delighting in pain, also he learned shrewdness and cunning; and soon he was accomplished at diverting hurt from himself to someone else. In sexual activities, where he was once the target he became the arrow, and on the vainly protesting forms of others, he discharged the venom of his frustration.

Thus, Charles did to others what had been done to him. The rejection by his mother, "being beaten unmercifully for the smallest infraction" by foster mothers and fathers, and other authority figures, and the transfer of his feelings of hatred on to Lindner, led to violent outbursts and unmanageable behavior.

To the next card (III), Charles says, "Two objects trying to pick something off the ground." At the end of the test the examiner asked Charles, "Could they be people?" He responded, "If they are people, they only have one leg." He was then asked, "What might they be picking up?" He responded, "Could be something in a bag."

Lindner had discovered by luck a very important sexual ritual and perversion that Charles repeatedly engaged in. When Lindner was "Officer of the Day" and had to distribute the drugs to the wards, Charles insisted on carrying the drug box for him, and opening it with the key, obviously stimulated by the box and the ritual. At one point, Charles put his whole hand into the box ("What the hell are you doing?") with the explanation, "I was just trying to see what's in the box." ("You know what's in the box and you know you're not supposed to fool with it"). This was the first time Lindner was actually frightened of Charles ("Sweat beaded his whole face, his breathing was rapid and shallow, his lips dry, his skin drawn in taut lines suggesting an extreme of tension''—''What do you want?''— ''The box, gimme the box.''—''Why?''—''I want to see what's in it''). The following morning Lindner emptied the box of drugs and replaced them with toys. He discovered that Charles had been searching for his mother's wedding ring (''Last night I could have sworn it was in the box'').

Although Lindner dates the time Charles first explored the trunk in his mother's room to age thirteen, there is evidence that Charles knew about the trunk and may have associated it with incestuous masturbation fantasies at age nine. It was to the trunk under the window that Charles ran when he was so excited over the prospect of sleeping with his mother. The trunk was mysterious, full of secrets, and he had to investigate its every compartment and all its contents over and over when he was alone. The odor of perfume from the trunk rendered him dizzy. When Charles explored his mother's trunk he was symbolically exploring, touching, feeling, smelling his mother (trunk = body, box = vagina, ring = vagina and illusory penis). It was the metal box with its bills, coins, pins, pearls, brooch and finally the wedding ring, which Charles always saved for last. It is interesting to note that Charles' job in the ward was custodian of the game closet. He ''beamed with pleasure'' when he accepted the key (''no hero ever received a medal more proudly than Charles accepting the key to the closet from our Head Attendant'').

Charles used his mother's ring for perverted practices. Father had given the ring to mother, she had worn it and so did Charles. Thus, he could identify with both parents in a symbolic primal scene. Lindner describes the perverted activity as follows:

> He took the ring in his hands, into it, one after another, he thrust each finger. Then he put the ring in his mouth, sliding his tongue into the circle. At last he held it against his quivering awakened sex.

Charles also needed the ring to obtain potency with the prostitute (he made her wear it). When his mother removed the money from the metal box, he went to her ''bag,'' to steal small sums so he could accumulate enough to visit a prostitute. It is interesting that the prostitute said to Charles, ''This is your first time, ain't it, Sonny. Well. . .it's a good thing you got me and not just any old bag. . .

Come here.'' Both the murder and attack on Lindner were preceded by a bell ringing following some severe frustration. It is possible that a bell was rung prior to his mother's leaving him at the end of visiting hours in one or more of the institutions. It seems that whether ring is used as a verb (to ring) or a noun (ring) the word was greatly disturbing to Charles.

The object on the Rorschach bending down could be Charles, the bag his mother (his wish to explore her, her bag or her box) or the prostitute, and brings to mind the entire perversion ritual. The fact that the figure has only one leg (also animals on Card VIII have only three legs), suggests the sense of castration and feelings of impotence Charles experienced. His sexual life was intimately related to his fixation on his mother, to the trunk, its contents, the box, and finally the ring, without which he was impotent. He felt like a man with a missing leg, castrated, and this would make him more paranoid and defensive, fearful of attack by others.

Lindner pointed out that after Charles disclosed his ''deepest and most intimate secret'' he became ''apathetic,'' ''unproductive,'' and Lindner interpreted this ''dull period'' as a ''natural, expected even lull.'' He wrote:

> A period of quiescence and recovery necessarily follows each high point in therapy. This permits the personality to assimilate its new insights and to reorient itself accordingly, and I felt that Charles was now in such an interim phase. Indeed (I thought as I hurried to the hospital), I had even exploited this period to strengthen the transference bonds between the boy and myself. Because I knew that the hurt of the past had to be undone, that he needed to feel wanted, appreciated, even loved before he could recover a sense of identity basic to the remaking of his personality. I have been more than usually permissive with him.

Lindner implied that the increased ''transference bonds'' were maternal and therefore had both positive (closeness) and negative (hate and rage) aspects. The only information we have concerning the attack on Lindner was that Charles had placed him in a maternal transference. We are told that when Charles touched Lindner's shoulder, it felt to him like a woman's breast and therefore Charles was attacking his mother by attacking Lindner as he had attacked the girl he murdered. Charles was probably realistically angry at Lindner for getting him to reveal his most precious possession, his masturbation fantasy and activity. During the episode in which Lindner unwisely permitted Charles to carry the metal narcotic box and Charles frightened Lindner enough for him to open it and display all its contents, there was considerable touching of Charles on Lindner's part. Although Lindner escaped attack on this occasion, he did not in the next confrontation between them. Charles was very emotionally upset and delusional, saying things like, "no, no," and "don't, don't," as if he were being done to. At this time Lindner put his hand on Charles' shoulder and placed his face on a level with Charles' face, when the telephone rang. Charles heard the voice in his head once again saying "kill, kill," and he choked Lindner, requiring several men to free Lindner and control Charles. Charles didn't know who he was and indeed probably didn't know who Lindner was at the time of the attack. Another possibility, for the attack not suggested by Lindner, was that Charles had a homosexual fixation on him which might have been fed by the excessive physical contact between them. Lindner probably would have wisely responded that this was all part of treating a severely deprived, affect-starved child. Thus, the "expected lull" described above could have been a kind of distancing of Lindner.

To the next card (IV) Charles saw "Skins off an animal" and in the inquiry said, "Two furs—another fur." There are two references to fur in Lindner's description of the case. The first is Charles' reference to "the thick softness of the fur coat" his mother wore when she visited him at the foster home, kissed him and he became dizzy and sick. The second reference related to Charles noticing the prostitute in the bar. She was hatless and "over her shoulders draped a short coat of fur." Charles was a sensuous person. He was in and out of his mother's closets, drawers, trunk, all over her room. He was particularly sensitive to odor, softness and feminine things. Although Lindner did not mention any fetishes, Charles' interest in his mother's possessions far exceeded normal interest. Lindner's descriptions of Charles turning back his mother's silk bedspread and running the tips of his fingers through it, the removal of the shawl and cushions covering the trunk, and the handling of the materials in the trunk, all suggest a strong sensuality and possibly the viewing of the silk and the ring as transitional objects.

It is not clear what upset Charles causing him to reject Card V. There are several possibilities. The fur responses to Card V and their connecting links may have disturbed him. When he saw an animal skin on Card VI, he was very careful to deny that he saw fur. The structure of Card V may have upset him. He denied that the "spread" on the card could be that of a bat, and said, a bat "doesn't have two feet here" (where women's feet are often seen). It is possible that he saw women's feet and the spread, which could have suggested sex and possibly the murder trauma of spreading the girl's legs apart in trying to penetrate her with his penis. When he failed at this attempt, he then penetrated her with his fingers. The spread could also refer to his mother's bedspread. The many projection responses on this card are often disturbing to patients (legs, tail, feet), although Piotrowski[14] as well as others point out that this card is the easiest to respond to. The upper phallic projection on Card VI (the sexual card) disturbed Charles. When the examiner asked if the top projection looked like anything, he became very self-derogatory and said, "I guess I'm stupid. . . What is a totem?" The totem response suggests the importance of the phallus to Charles, as well as his need to deny its importance. It was as if he were saying, "I'm stupid, I'm innocent, I don't know anything."

Charles' responses to the mother card (VII) are similar to those he offered to Card I ("clouds" and again "a river"). These responses suggest Charles' evasiveness, anxiety, and a diffuseness or vagueness of perception. Charles' strong unconscious wish to reunite with his mother, to seek the passivity of an intra-uterine existence, or even death, and thus merge with his mother, meant giving up any sense of self and autonomy.

In Card VIII Charles saw "Two animals of an unknown nature" that became "Wild animals" in the inquiry, and then "Two heads of something" that became "Prehistoric animals back in Adam and Eve's time."

Piotrowski[14] writes, "The non-human responses provide an approximate measure of the degree of imperfect integration and an indication of what the behavior of the individual is likely to be when he acts in a state of markedly lessened integration." Thus he postulates a correlation between the quality of non-human movement and overt behavior in states of diminished consciousness and offers the following hypothesis:

> . . . if any of an individual's FM (animal movement) is more assertive, active or expansive than any of his M (human movement), he is likely—provided he behaves criminally at times— to commit an aggressive criminal act against a person (and per-

haps property as well) in a state of diminished consciousness.

Let us first look at Charles' human movement and then at his animal movement responses to see his propensity for acting out.

Charles' one human movement response to Card III is blocked as the "objects" are "trying to pick up something" and therefore are not definitely successful in their task. Thus, the tendency toward compliance is somewhat modified by a secondary and much weaker tendency toward assertiveness, which in turn is blocked. To Piotrowski[14], often such patients seek a benevolent and stronger person on whom to lean. The main objective may be assertion, but the inability to succeed suggests "severe inner inhibitions which interfere with self-assertiveness." Charles' human movement is blocked and would seem to indicate marked and deep-seated indecisiveness.

Lindner was puzzled by Charles' two-year stay on the farm without incident. However he did say, "Charles was tractable and mild in his institutional life. With the ward patients he showed great consideration, even tenderness." The Michaux and Michaux report[13], based on Charles' behavior over the next thirteen years, pointed out Charles' diligence, meticulousness, conformity, devotion to duty and fine display of ambition and conscientious effort. He won the praise of the prison authorities who commented, "We have always found him to be reliable, trustworthy, a diligent worker, and above all, possessing the desire to do a good job"[13].

Charles' animal movement responses (animals fighting or kissing to Card II, a gorilla who Charles would "sure hate to meet up with" to Card IV, and wild and prehistoric animals to Card VIII) contain a good deal of aggression. This suggests that the sadistic push is deeply embedded and is indeed at the core of his personality structure. When we add to the animal responses the highly unstable, emotionally labile, strongly impulsive, uninhibited self-centered color response with utter disregard for other peoples' rights to Card IX, we see the tendency toward sudden unpredictable outbursts of brutality. After an unusual delay to Card IX (300 seconds), Charles said, "Yeah, mumbo, jumbo, like a child takes paint and throws it." Charles' handling of movement resembles the pattern of sexual offenders reported by Piotrowski[15].

Lindner probably would never have administered sodium pentathol if he had given Charles a Rorschach before he saw him. After Charles was transferred from the medical ward to the psychiatric ward, following an appendectomy, Lindner saw him every day and got nowhere with him. Charles was unable to free associate, seemed to lack depth, functioned strictly in the here and now describing his daily activities, didn't seem capable of a positive or negative transference, reacted automatically without emotional involvement and sealed off the past. It was at this point that Lindner decided to use the drug. The sodium pentathol interview brought out details of the murder and that Charles had heard a voice which told him to kill. Although Charles did not become violent at this time, Lindner later stated that hypnosis or narco-synthesis were not the treatment of choice as Charles had too much rage and Lindner was afraid to risk the precipitation of a psychotic episode.

That Charles saw wild, prehistoric or archaic animals to the first all-colored Rorschach card should not surprise us as he was extremely threatened by his environment. "Wild" and "a veritable monster" is the way Lindner saw Charles. He wrote:

> This orphaned, rejected, deprived boy represented a clear instance of utter personal distortion consequent upon denial to a child of all it requires for psychological growth. The total frustration of his deepest affectional needs produced an emotionally starved individual. Those dreadful events of life in homes and orphanages, acting upon the original twist given his personality, compounded the basic deformation of character, and upon this rotten foundation had been added layer after layer of further distortion—until he became, at adolescence, a veritable monster who could obtain satisfaction for his instincts and needs only through violence, perversion and destruction.
>
> For me, it was like looking into a deep pit where wild and hungry animals howled for release.

Lindner's experience with Charles bears out the implications of Charles' explosive paint throwing response. After getting nowhere with Charles for a period of time, Lindner discovered Charles playing with chess and checker men while engrossed and talking out loud. Lindner then decided that the preferred method of treatment for Charles would be play therapy. In one instance Charles upset a pot of glue on Lindner's desk and after wiping up its sticky content left one spot of glue on the desk. Lindner pointed it out to Charles, who said, "You make me sick, just like my mother." Lindner took "sick" literally and this led to Charles' association to his mother as making him sick and his sexual involvement with her. Lindner, in describing Charles' play activity, wrote:

> My office became a shambles as jars were overturned, paint spilled, dolls broken, fires were lit, and toys destroyed by "accidents." As for me, on my head fell torrents of abuse.

> So all the privations Charles had known were now laid upon me, and into our daily meetings there flowed a continuous torrent of complaint, blame, and indictment fed by streams from the past. Not only to release his aggressivity, but also to test my patience and—yes—my love. Charles destroyed almost every object I brought into our work.

Charles' second response to Card IX was, "Two unidentified objects—couldn't call it a human head." In the test proper Charles felt the objects were more of an "animal nature," while in the inquiry he felt the objects were "more human." This indecision, denial and lack of certainty (to know who and what he is) has already been commented on. Charles' inability to identify percepts clearly, to be vague, non-committal, and critical of himself runs throughout the entire Rorschach. Lindner did a splendid job in pointing out the lack of identity, animal-human confusion (tendency toward depersonalization), and the excessive doubt.

After 600 seconds, Card X was seen as an "object." Charles then says, "I don't know what these green things are—two—." He sees "The face of a rabbit," followed by "The green things take it away—cover the eyes." He denies that the green things are part of the rabbit's head.

It is interesting that Charles started the test with a top center response and finished with a bottom center response. If we consider the center or midline to be mother or the pull toward mother, then he both begins and ends with her. The rabbit's head and the green things which are often seen as caterpillars are both frequently perceived responses. A patient's proclivity to combine these disparate and incongruous elements reflects a tendency toward loose and disturbed thinking. This is actually Charles' only combined response (he had been very careful to be vague and indefinite) and it is one that appears quite frequently in the records of paranoid patients (caterpillars or worms eating at the eyes of a rabbit; a green discharge coming from the eyes). The content itself suggests various possibilities, depending on the patient's elaboration and affect.

(*Jack Rabbit*—virile, potent, active, productive; *rabbit*—scared, fearful, timid, harmless; *bunny*—cuddly, soft, playful, cute, curvy, seductive; *Bugs Bunny*—defiant, sadistic, smart-alecky, voracious). Many interpretations are possible: the wish to cover the eyes, not to see or know; to forget or push away from conscious awareness (trauma); the wish to look at and destroy with the symbolic eye or to devour with the eye, and the talion punishment (an eye for an eye) that accompanies such wishes. According to Fenichel[2], the eye is a phallic symbol and to be blinded (to cover up the eyes) is to be castrated, "which is the punishment for some transgression prompted by the scoptophilic impulse."

Lindner discusses in great detail Charles' scoptophilic tendencies (the compulsion to look into his mother's bag, drawers, closet, boxes, trunk, bathroom). Charles had the need to carry out these compulsions and there was guilt as well as excitement attached to the acts.

Summary

The Rorschach of Charles, a teen-age sex murderer, was presented in light of Lindner's analysis of the case. Robert Lindner had a strong belief in and devotion to Rorschach content and this paper is a tribute to him. There are many quotes from his story, *Songs My Mother Taught Me,* for the passages linger on, as the sensitivity, integrity and clinical acumen of the man remains indelibly imprinted on all those who read his words.

BIBLIOGRAPHY

1. Bleuler, E. (1924): *Textbook of Psychiatry.* New York: The Macmillan Co.

2. Fenichel, O. (1953): The Scoptophilic Instinct and Identification. *Collected Papers of Otto Fenichel.* Vol. 1. New York: Norton and Co.

3. Freud, S. (1920): Beyond the Pleasure Principle. *Standard Edition,* XVIII. London: Hogarth Press, 1955.

4. Lindner, R.M. (1944): Some Significant Rorschach Responses. *J. Crim. Psychopath.,* 5:775-778.

5. ————(1946): Content Analysis in Rorschach Work. *Rorschach Res. Exch.,* 10:121-129.

6. ————(1947): Analysis of the Rorschach Test by Content. *J. Crim. Psychopath.,* 8:707-719.

7. ————(1948): The Equivalents of Matricide. *Psa. Quart.,* 17:453-470.

8. ————(1950): The Content Analysis of the Rorschach Protocol. In: *Projective Psychology: Clinical Approaches to the Total Personality.* Eds. L.E. Abt and L. Bellak. New York: Knopf Inc.

9. ————(1955): The Clinical Use of Content Analysis in Rorschach Testing. *Psychoanalysis,* 3:12-17.

10. ————(1955): *The Fifty Minute Hour.* New York: Holt, Rinehart and Winston, Inc.

11. ————(1982): *The Fifty Minute Hour.* Jason Aronson Inc.

12. Lindner, R.M. and Seliger, R.V. (1946): Content Analysis in Rorschach Work; *Amer. Psychol.,* 1:286-287.

13. Michaux, M.H. and Michaux, W.W. (1963): Psychodiagnostic Follow-up of a Juvenile Sex Murderer. *Psychoanal. Rev.,* 50:93-112.

14. Piotrowski, Z.A. (1957): *Perceptanalysis.* New York: The Macmillan Co.

15. Piotrowski, Z.A. and Abrahamson, D. (1952): Sexual Crime, Alcohol and the Rorschach Test. *Psychiat. Quart.,* Volume 26.

16. Schafer, R. (1954): *Psychoanalytic Interpretation in Rorschach Testing.* New York: Grune and Stratton Co.